Book of Hope

Book of Hope

Stories of love, courage and recovery from families who have battled eating disorders

With artwork by Parry Scott & Penny Wooding and photographs by Eileen Sproule, Jenny Hawkins, Penny Wooding & Nancy Critchley

Sue Huff

H

First published by Sue Huff in 2014
Edmonton, Alberta, Canada

Library and Archives Canada Cataloguing in Publication

Huff, Sue, author
    Book of Hope: stories of love, courage and recovery from families
    who have battled eating disorders/Sue Huff; with artwork by
    Parry Wyminga Scott & Penny Wooding and photographs by
    Eileen Sproule, Jenny Hawkins, Penny Wooding & Nancy Critchley.

ISBN 978-0-9940001-0-1 (pbk.)

1. Eating disorders in adolescence—Patients—Biography. 2. Eating
disorders in adolescence—Patients—Family relationships. 3. Parent and
child. 4. Caregivers. 1. Title.

RJ506.E18H84 2015   616.85'2600835   C2015-900205-2

Book design by Susan Colberg

The writing of this book was made possible by a grant from the
Alberta Foundation for the Arts

For Hannah, of course
Kevin and Josh, always

Contents

Glossary of terms

Anorexia (chapters: Cassie, Julia, Hailey, Emma, Jenn)
The diagnostic criteria for anorexia, according to the American Psychiatric Association, includes "a refusal to maintain body weight at or above normal weight for age and height, intense fear of gaining weight, disturbance in the way in which one's body weight is experienced and the absence of three menstrual cycles". These criteria are not hard and fast for children and adolescents.

Addictions (chapters: Hailey, Sarah)
Addiction is the continued repetition of a behavior despite adverse consequences. It is estimated that as many as 50% of people who struggle with eating disorders are also involved in drug or alcohol abuse.

Antipsychotics
A class of drugs developed to treat schizophrenia which are also used to treat eating disorders, particularly during weight restoration, as they help reduce obsessionality and anxiety by blocking dopamine receptors in the brain.

BMI
Body Mass Index. It is not a measure of health, rather a number derived by comparing one's height and weight. BMI should not be considered the sole indicator/criteria of the presence/absence of an eating disorder.

CBT
Cognitive Behaviour Therapy. A goal-oriented therapy that divides eating disorder treatment into three overlapping phases: resisting urges through under-

standing the dangers, adjusting eating and preventing relapse. Evidence indicates it is very helpful in treating bulimia in adults.

Close (band or supervision)

The patient is not permitted to leave the treatment facility, unsupervised, either because they are still under evaluation or because their illness is too severe.

Cutting

Self-mutilation is often an expression of anxiety, depression or extreme emotional pain. The infliction of wounds creates a short burst of adrenaline which may bring short-term relief from the overwhelming feelings. Cutting can be very distressing to family members, however most wounds are superficial and should not to be confused with a suicide attempt.

DBT

Dialectical Behaviour Therapy. This type of therapy sees emotional regulation as the underlying problem. It focuses on learning new skills to regulate negative emotion and replacing dysfunctional or maladaptive behaviour with more healthy coping strategies.

Effexor

A medication sometimes used to treat depression/anxiety.

Ensure

The brand name of a meal replacement calorie-boosting drink.

fMRI

Functional Magnetic Resonance Imaging. Using a magnetic field, fMRIs take detailed pictures of the brain, showing changes in blood flow and oxygen, as the patient experiences various stimuli. fMRIs have provided a wealth of information about how eating disorders affect the brain.

OCD (chapter: Cassie)

Obsessive Compulsive Disorder. It is characterized by obsessive intrusive thoughts and compulsive rituals, like skin picking or the need to touch objects in a particular order. The rituals are developed as a means to try and keep the obsessive thoughts from taking over.

PET

Positron Emission Tomography. Another type of brain scan that looks at chemicals in the brain, like serotonin and dopamine.

Pro-ana sites

Internet sites that, alarmingly, encourage eating disorder lifestyles.

Prozac

An anti-depressant. Clinical name: *Fluoxetine.* In weight-restored patients, research indicates fluoxetine may decrease relapse episodes and has been associated with better maintenance of weight.

Purging

Self-induced vomitting, misuse of laxatives, diuretics or enemas to rid the body of calories that have been ingested. Calories may also be purged through compulsive and excessive exercising, which is often harder to recognize in our fitness-supporting society.

Restricting

Reducing the number of calories ingested to a level which is not sufficient to meet the body's needs and results in rapid weight loss.

Refeeding (or weight restoration)

The process of gaining weight in order to return the body to a healthy weight. Refeeding can be physically very painful as the stomach is stretched and the digestive system is re-engaged, often causing gastic pain, constipation, bloating and other unpleasant physical sensations. Emotionally, refeeding can be even more painful, as every ounce gained can be accompanied by a pound of anxiety and disress. Therefore, refeeding needs to be conducted in a nurturing emotional context with realistic targets. (0.5–1 lb per week outside of a hospital setting, 2–3 lbs for hospitalizied patients).

The Unit (or 4F4)

The Eating Disorder Clinic, located on the fourth floor at the University of Alberta Hospital in Edmonton. Treatment is offered as an outpatient, day patient or inpatient, based on the severity of the illness and family/patient preference.

Timeline

November 12: First interview for the book

November 13: Hannah eats first food outside home/hospital—
frozen yoghurt

December 1: Successfully eating lunches with friends at school

December 6: First supper at home. This breaks 7 months of driving
to the hospital every day

2013

January 30: Last interview for the book completed

February 7: Hannah officially discharged from hospital

April 16: I discover a lump

April 25: Biopsy

May 2: Breast cancer confirmed

May 25: Hannah relapses, admitted as full-time patient

June 5: Surgery at Cross Cancer Institute

June 30: Hannah finishes Grade 9 at hospital school

August 15: Hannah released from hospital

August 29: Last day of radiation treatment

October 5: I start a new job

2014

June 28: Hannah finishes Grade 10 at her school, 1st time since
Grade 7

July 18: I get the one year "all clear" from my doctor

July 23: Eating Disorder Support Network of Alberta receives three-year
funding from provincial government to offer support groups

August: Hannah goes away with friends to a camp in Victoria

October: EDSNA support groups start

2015

January: *Book of Hope* published

Introduction

When it finally hit me how sick our daughter was, I almost collapsed. We had just come from a doctor's appointment, (the second in eight days) and it was suddenly crystal clear how rapid and uncontrolled her weight loss was. She wanted to go back to school after the appointment and somehow I managed to drive her there. As soon as she was out of sight, I started crying. By the time I got home, I was shaking uncontrollably, my lips were numb, I couldn't feel my fingertips and I wasn't sure if my legs would carry me up the steps. When I got inside the house, I immediately called my sister, but all I could get out was: "She's so sick!!!" My sister dropped everything and came over. In addition to being my sibling, she was also my office manager and, somehow, we developed a plan to get through the final two weeks of my election campaign. I had been campaigning as a provincial candidate for ten months and, by this point, over a hundred volunteers had joined me. I felt I had to continue to cross the finish line, but those last two weeks of the campaign were a blur of confusion, exhaustion and just-below-the-surface panic.

My husband and I didn't know what to do. We didn't understand anorexia; we had no point of reference. Luckily, a friend put us in direct contact with Dr. Lara Ostolosky at the Eating Disorder Clinic (also known as Unit 4F4) at the University of Alberta. When we met "Dr. O", as she is called, all three of us immediately felt calmer. We knew we had found the person who would lead us out of the wilderness.

The journey of refeeding and weight restoration was intense and painful for our daughter. The journey for us, as parents, was traumatic, confusing and lonely. Once the initial panic subsided, I felt a yearning for stories of other parents who had "been there, done that". And, more than anything, I needed to hear stories of recovery.

I went looking for hope. When I couldn't find the book I needed, I decided to create it. I had never written a book before and really had no idea how much work would be involved, but I had worked in the documentary style in television, film, theatre and radio. Aside from all that, I was desperate.

Dr. Ostolosky kindly agreed to send out a letter to her former patients, letting them know about my desire to collect stories from families who had walked the path of recovery and create a book of hope for all who face this illness. My contact information was provided in the letter and families were invited to email me if they were willing to connect and share. Nine families bravely stepped forward. They invited me into their kitchens and living rooms, shared their stories (and their *Kleenex*) with me. It was a remarkable and powerful experience, one that I hope to pay forward in some small measure by sharing this book.

• A few notes about the book

The names of the participants have been changed. Some families wanted anonymity, some didn't care, but more than simply protecting privacy and creating an environment where it was safer to share, I wanted to avoid feeding prejudices about families with eating disorders. With a name, a profession, or a description of a home, the reader might be tempted to make assumptions about who is affected by eating disorders and who is immune. I consciously left out details of cultural background, physical build, occupation, hair colour, economic status or race because I want to challenge any preconceptions that may exist and emphasize the "everyman" quality of this illness. Eating disorders can affect your co-worker, your child, your neighbour, your sister, your boyfriend or you. Quite likely, there are people in your life who are currently battling an undiagnosed or untreated eating disorder.

Secondly, I wanted the stories to be captured in the most authentic way possible. So I recorded all the interviews and transcribed them, verbatim. I have edited the interviews for length, clarity and narrative flow, but I have not embellished or rewritten their words. I felt it was important to allow the families to tell their stories, without commentary, interpretation or judgement. Each family's perspective is entirely their own and therefore the stories, on occasion, contradict each other. This diversity of experience is, I hope, a source of strength and inspiration rather than confusion. It underlines the fact that there are many routes to recovery and it is important to keep trying until you find the path that works for you.

Finally, during the interviews, participants often referred to their lowest weight or the amount of weight they lost, but I have removed all the numbers and replaced them with an "X". I did this out of respect for anyone reading this book who is currently struggling with an eating disorder and may feel challenged, compelled or triggered by numbers as targets. I also didn't want family members to use numbers as a comparison point for their child's illness and underestimate the seriousness of an eating disorder that does not have significant weight loss. I'll admit: I was tempted to include the weights to emphasize how devastating and life-threatening this illness can be, but I trust that the stories will adequately convey that point without numbers, because we are so much more than numbers.

• This is a book built on hope

For those who battle eating disorders, I hope you see yourself in these stories and draw comfort, knowing you are not alone. I hope you will reach out fearlessly like Olivia and say: "I need help". I hope the stories will inspire you to believe that recovery is possible and to remember that no matter how dark it looks today, there is light ahead.

For the family members who walk this difficult path, I hope you will gain insight, comfort, resilience and strength by reading these stories. I hope you will fight the demon of shame and connect with others. By sharing your experience, you will help break the stigma and ignorance surrounding mental illness and lead us all to a more compassionate society.

For those who know very little about eating disorders, I hope these stories will increase your understanding and diminish your judgement. I hope you will reach out to those who are affected and say: "I don't know what to do or say, but I'm here." Your kindness, ability to listen and steadfast friendship are the greatest gifts you can give to families facing an eating disorder.

For professionals working in the medical field, I hope this book will inform and improve the way you treat eating disorders in your office, clinic or hospital. I hope it will shed light on the many and profound ways that family members are impacted and that it will encourage you to improve your services for them, as well. About five months into our daughter's treatment, I said, "If you don't start providing more support for me, you'll have another patient in your system very quickly." It turns out those were prophetic words, as is revealed later in this book.

• Thank you, thank you, thank you

First of all, of course, thank you to all the families who had the courage to share their stories in the hopes of helping other families. I was humbled by your trust and inspired by your generosity. Each story provided a new insight and every family gave me hope that one day we would be whole again.

Thank you Dr. O and the all the treatment professionals at the Eating Disorder Clinic at the University of Alberta Hospital (4F4). Thank you for the patience, dedication and determination you show, day in and day out, in the face of this incredibly complex illness. You save lives and we all owe you a tremendous debt.

Thank you to my dear friends—Eileen, Toby and Karen—who stayed by me through all the hard days and never stopped believing we'd get there. Thanks to Andrea at *Acupuncture Works* for healing my broken heart.

Thank you to Susan Colberg for the beautiful book and cover design. Her professional skill is evident throughout this book and I am eternally grateful for her contribution. Thank you to everyone who patiently (and sometimes tearfully) read versions; provided constructive feedback; supplied photographs/artwork or helped to shape this book and steward its publication. Thank you to Dianne Drummond, who kindly proofed the research sections of the book and offered encouragement. Any errors that remain are entirely mine.

Finally, thank you to my family for supporting the writing of this book and for bravely walking the path of recovery, hand-in-hand.

PHOTO: JENNY HAWKINS

Cassie

Cassie was 18 years old at the time of the interview.
Her eating disorder started when she was 14 years old.

"I did it to make the world seem perfect in my eyes
rather than face the reality of my life."

"[The eating disorder] was my safe haven."

Cassie: I don't like seeing other girls going through what I went through.
I wanted to give back and help other girls. And to help me share my story.
I think a sign of recovering is when you expose it, to actually say, "I have
an eating disorder" and not hide it.

I don't even know how it started. I guess, the whole self-esteem thing, in
Grade 9. It started little and then it kept progressing, progressing.

For me, it was all about control. My family was starting to fall apart. My
mom was going off in her direction, back to her eating disorder and back
to drugs. I didn't like seeing the family break apart. Everyone was off in
their own direction. There wasn't balance in the house. It was chaos. Coming home every day, chaos at school... me being able control of that aspect
of my life [eating], made me feel like I have control of my life and that
everything was going perfectly, when really it wasn't. So I did it to make
the world seem perfect in my eyes rather than face the reality of life. [The
eating disorder] was my safe haven.

My parents were in Red Deer, getting their divorce thing and I was home alone and I was tired of being a problem, so I tried to make myself eat what I thought was a lot. It caused me to freak out and I had a... heart murmur? And they found me on the floor and I got sent to the Stollery [Children's Hospital cardiac ward] for about two weeks. And then transferred over to the [Eating Disorder] Unit.

I was the first one to trash Dr. P's office. He told me I had to be "X" lbs and I didn't like being that [target weight]; in my mind, I wanted to be "X-1" lbs. So I flipped over his bookcase. I just went a totally different personality than who I was. Thankfully, Dr. O agreed that I could be "X-1" lbs, which was a big deal to me and I'm thankful she did, because I don't think I would be in the program [otherwise]. It was a struggle at first, but over time I decided I can't really fight it, I might as well try and get better and have a life.

• How would you describe your path to recovery?

I didn't like recovery at first. It was a fight to get me to go. To me, it meant nothing at first. I just thought it was like a joke: I wasn't going to do this. There's no way. And then slowly, once your mind starts working better, you begin to think more, and wonder: "Why you are doing this? And do you really want to live that way?" And my mom always had that problem [with an eating disorder] and I pictured myself: "Do I always want to be falling back like my mother did or do I want to actually have a life and make something of it?"

The nurses helped me to overcome that. They were really nice and easy to talk to and stuff like that and the same with Dr. O, too. The program was great, but it did take me a couple of months to come out of my shell. I didn't want anyone to touch me. I was closed off, shut out from the world, so absorbed in the eating disorder. I wanted to be alone, just my own little self. I was angry. Mad that I'm here. It was hard, frustrating.

[The Unit] was scary: the locking of the doors, it was an eye-opener! When I went on the Unit, I was 14. It was kind of hard at first. The adults were intimidating. I used to love going to the Stollery School [school at the hospital]. I didn't want to leave. The teachers were so nice. It was fun. It was a break. You didn't think about [the eating disorder]. Just do your school work. I loved it there. You got to open up and be yourself there.

With your roommates [on the Unit] you can see how far you've come [compared] to what they're doing. I remember thinking: "I would have been in that situation three or four months ago and it's not really worth it." You can see them hurting themselves, them hurting others and you ask, "Why would I want to do that?"

There's a lot of questioning: Who you are? What you want? Why are you doing this? I think how stupid to trash [Dr. P's] office over one pound! What was I doing? Looking back at that stuff.

One of the hardest things was telling my friends that I wasn't really in the hospital because my heart wasn't working, that I actually had an eating disorder. I didn't do that until the end of recovery. I let them believe, I let my whole family believe... only my close family—my parents and my sister—knew I was actually in there for an eating disorder. When you have an eating disorder, you want to keep it secret. You don't want anyone else knowing who you are. You are in your own little world.

But the hardest part was actually learning to eat, being comfortable with what you eat, realizing you can eat junk food, you can be healthy, don't need to think about calories, you can exercise properly and don't overdo it. And to actually admit you have a problem.

• What helped you overcome the relapses?

I've had one or two relapses within the past four years. I've gotten over them with the help of my family. Eating disorders don't go away, there will always be a part in your mind. Nobody's going to have a perfect recovery. There's going to be off days. There's gonna be relapses but you just have to fight to get through it. There's another day.

Afterwards, I always make myself think: "Is it really worth it, Cassie? Why are you doing this? It's just one little mistake. We don't have to make this day count for all your years [of hard work]." I would think to calm myself.

Ask myself questions. Or go for a walk. Down to the river and sit there and think. Talking to a person that you are able to talk to (helps). Or your friends that you trust. You want to hear that people care for you.

A lot of people [with ED] are scared of losing people, because they get so much attention [while they are sick]. If you are back to normal, does everything change? Do you have the same relationship with people? [When you are sick] people are always concerned with you, your well-being, they want to spend time with you, they want to do all those things. Obviously, people who are self-conscious are going to think that will all disappear when they get back to normal, when they find their balance. That's hard: trying to find your balance in recovery, where you are just happy.

• Hope

I started to have hope half-way through. The hope was just to find my true self and to find happiness in life. And to actually have a purpose, like fulfill things, not waste my life.

Sue: Did anyone give you hope?

Cassie: I'm not really too sure. I think it had to do with myself. Making my own hope.

Sue: I like that: "making your own hope." How did you do that?

Cassie: I dunno... just determining your values, your beliefs, who you are, what you want to do, what you want to accomplish. And not focusing it on someone else. Just do it for yourself. You could do it for your mom or do it for your dad, but it's not going to work, it's not going to have the same result as if you do it for yourself.

• Resilience

Where does it come from? Probably from my stubborn nature. I can be really stubborn. If I don't want to do things, I'm not going to do them. 'Cuz before, I was determined to have control of my life. But through recovery, I was determined to get better and I put all my focus into that rather than harming myself.

• Turning points

Well, I decided, after I got back [home], I wasn't going to go after terrible boyfriends. (*laughs*) You know what I mean... the guys into drugs and smoking and treating girlfriends like crap and stuff like that, so I didn't date for a long time. I didn't want just another boyfriend. In junior high, all girls need to have a boyfriend just the need to say, "Yeah, I've got a boyfriend." When I got back, I thought I don't need to have a boyfriend. A boyfriend will come when I'm ready. So I got rid of that aspect of my life. Now, with guys, I know, they have a great wall they have to take down before they get to see me. Just because of my past and stuff like that, I don't trust guys. So I guess knowing where I stand with relationships [was a turning point]. You don't need it to define who you are.

I always used to hang out with the popular crowd, but, after my experience, I ditched a bunch of my friends, got new friends. I started talking to people I would never had talked to [before] and they are the greatest people. I'm glad I did that. They are actually my good friends, they are there for me, care for me, rather than the whole drama. I'm sticking with my true friends and staying away from the back-stabbers.

So instead of partying every weekend and hanging out with my friends who were into that stuff, it will just be one or two times, with my good friends. Being able to experience life, but not get sucked into it. I'm able to still party and hang out with my friends, but I'm also still getting good grades, going to school, bettering my education. I'm finding balance in my life.

My dad... Slowly towards the end, I decided to forgive him. I realized he wasn't the bad person I thought he was, just because he was trying to care for me. I used to hate my dad, because he was the one who wanted to get me better. I wouldn't talk to him. I used to hate his guts, but now I'm really close with my dad. We've come a long way. My mom... I don't have contact with my mom. She helped when I was in the hospital, but as I was getting better, she was not. She spiralled right down. She's living in Vancouver on East Hastings Street. It was best not to have contact, but I hope I have contact with her when she's all better, because she's still my mom. So my dad is raising both of us and that's made us closer because he's like the mom and the dad. He does a lot for us.

I always used to be a really angry child. When I wouldn't get my way, it would be bad. One of the things contributing to my eating disorder was also my OCD. 'Cuz of OCD, I had to do things in a routine. Everything had to be in a routine. My eating disorder had to be in a routine and it furthered it. My OCD has cut back a bit, which is good. I take medication for that and I'm more happy with life. I was on antidepressants for a while and I'm starting to cut back. I'm almost done. I don't think I need them anymore.

I'm more caring, more understanding now. I don't get angry or act out when I shouldn't be. I know myself way better: what I like, what I don't like, what's important, what's not. And how to act towards people. I've learned that everyone is different in their own way and they are beautiful in their own way. That it's better to face reality than try to avoid it in the long run, because there's going to be big consequences if you avoid it. Being able to open up with people more and being able to be myself, and know who I am, has helped a lot.

• Life now

It's pretty good. I'm going to Costa Rica on spring break with my dad and sister, saving up with my own money. My dad wants us to learn how to save our own money. I just bought a new car. Everything is going good right now. It is starting to come together.

I'm finishing Grade 12, hoping to go to Calgary [for post-secondary]. I'm still thinking what I want to go into. I think I'm going to be a medical office assistant. I really want to be a psychologist, which I might take after my medical office assistant. I've always wanted to give back. I thought about being a counsellor in junior high. You can personally relate: I'm not just some person that just went to school and knows nothing about it. Dr. O, she told me she used to have one [an eating disorder], and that helped me to relate to her more. Knowing she was in the same position, helped me open up more. That's helped a lot with my recovery too: thinking she's not just another person who's getting paid.

[Having an eating disorder] was living hell but it helped me find that there is a brighter side to everything. There is hope and belief. I'm not going back to my eating disorder. The key is to surround yourself with people that love you and focus on things that you love to do.

You just have to start to believe and accept yourself.

Since the interview, Cassie has completed high school, had a wonderful trip to Costa Rica, completed her course as a medical assistant and is now working at her local hospital.

RESEARCH SAYS

"No evidence exists to prove that families cause eating disorders. Furthermore, blaming family members harms their psychological well-being...rather, the point is to identify family stressors whose amelioration may facilitate recovery."

— *Practice Guideline for the Treatment of Patients with Eating Disorders* Third Edition, American Psychiatric Association, 2006

PHOTO: SUE HUFF

Jack (Cassie's dad)

"It's scary. Even doctors... doctors don't even know enough about this!"

"Having to leave her in Edmonton, at that age, all by herself and drive away, it's so hard because you want to wrap your arms around them and pretend it's going to be OK, but it's not. It was brutal— driving away."

Jack: I think the biggest reason I agreed to participate [in this book] is because my daughter has always wanted to give back and I know when we were going through this, there was not enough information. There isn't enough information out there for parents. Too many people don't want to admit that there's a problem. They think it will go away, but it won't go away, it just gets worse.

It's scary, even doctors... doctors don't even know enough about this! Because when Cassie initially started having all the heart problems and her heart rate went down to 32 beats a minute, I remember being in the hospital in Rocky [Mountain House, Alberta] and we kept saying, "She's got an eating disorder" and the doctors had no idea what we were talking about. It's scary. I remember being very firm with one doctor and saying, "No, we need to get her to Edmonton." He had no clue about the eating disorder clinics in Edmonton and the one in Calgary—we had to educate the doctors. We just about lost her; it scared the living daylights out of me.

- ## How would you describe the journey?

(*laughs*) That's a tough one. To be honest, the last four years have been such a blur because of everything that we've been through. I was going through a divorce at that time too, so there was so much going on. There was a ton of chaos. I still look back and go "What was that??!" It's been brutal. There were so many emotions. You'd cry. I was scared, scared for my daughter, scared I was going to lose her. That was the biggest one. I kept focused on my children and making sure that everybody was going to be okay.

- ## What were the hardest parts for you?

The hardest thing for me was when Cassie was so angry and she was taking everything out on me. Everybody's got to have an outlet and I understood that. They say if they lash out on you, it's because they love you and they know you're safe, and that's why, I think, she did it.

I remember one day we were in Red Deer we were going to *Booster Juice* and I remember Cassie getting so angry. She was trying to get out of the truck and I was holding her back and saying, "No, Cassie, you can't." Cassie was going to attack her mom. She was so angry. It wasn't her fault. Her mind wasn't thinking properly. It's all those serotonin levels and all that. [The anorexic rages] are scary. She attacked me that day. She kicked me in the face, she punched me in the face, she bit me so hard she drew blood on my arm. She was sick, but I didn't know... I thought it was everything else that was going on in our lives with the divorce. I was kind of in the dark. I was trying to save the family still, I wasn't paying enough attention to Cassie.

And having to leave her in Edmonton [at the hospital], at that age, all by herself and drive away. It was brutal: driving away. I remember also having to be so firm and saying, "No. You need to go." And it's so hard because you want to wrap your arms around them and pretend it's going to be okay, but it's not. With Cassie's heart condition, we were in the Stollery [Hospital] cardiac ward for a bit. I remember the nurses saying, "You are the one that's gotta make these decisions. Stand your ground, and don't let her go home, because she will die." It's amazing what a person can do, when you are put in situations like that.

It was such a blur, going through that. It's hard to remember everything. Going to work early, work all day, driving to Edmonton three/four times a week because I wanted her to know I was there for her: Even though it's tough, no matter what, I love you, I will always be there for you. Being consistent meant a lot, I do believe.

Going to visit her for two hours, to help her to pull through, reassuring her... and then having to leave her again, every time, and drive away. It was brutal. You do what you gotta do. It doesn't matter if you had two hours' sleep. You get up and you do it. Yup.

It consumes your life. There were numerous times where I wanted to give up and my neighbour, the one that helped us through a lot of this, she kept saying to us, "You can't give up. You can't give up." Some days it would have been easier to put your hands up in the air and walk away, but you can't. As a parent, you can't. I knew that I couldn't crash. I knew that. I think that's part of what pulled me through too. I knew if I gave up, then she would give up. And there was no giving up. Constantly getting up every morning and putting one foot in front of the other. "Okay, I'm going to work. Okay I'm driving to Edmonton" It was one foot in front of the other.

It's hard. You have to continue to work. I started another job—I had to have two jobs—but what I found was by me going back to the body shop and contracting to them, I was able to focus on something different and it put me in a different place. I have a really good friend who works there, so when we're working on a Friday night, we're hanging out, we're having a couple of beers and talking and that's what pulled me through: focusing on something different. I was working, but still, it was a break.

• Where did you draw your strength from?

Just the love for my daughter. I'm a very, very strong family man. I believe in my kids, my morals, everything. I can't give up. I don't know where that came from. Even today, after everything has finally starting to slow down in our lives, I look back and think, 'How did I do that?' and you don't even know yourself. You just do it. The body is an amazing thing. But the past couple of years, I've gone on more trips. I'm taking more time for myself. I'll go sit on the beach and that's my recharge time. That's my time. Your body will tell it's when it's done: "You better have a nap" and I'll sleep for sometimes, 12 hours.

My parents, they've really pulled me through. My mom, (typically Dutch lady: "You eat. Eat. Eat."), she always made sure we had food. Mom and Dad, they are quite a bit older, so you can't really talk to them about a lot of things because they don't really understand it, but you know that they are there. My sister, Karen, she's been there also. Her husband passed away from bone marrow cancer—I think he was only 32—so my sister had been through a lot, too. So I was able to go to her place, sit down, drink coffee, just visit... and talk. Just being there. She had an understanding of what I was going through: the pain. My neighbours, Jane and Tim, they've been amazing for both my girls.

• Hope

I think the big thing was I knew that Cassie could make it and that she'd be able to survive it because of what my ex-wife had gone through: she had had an eating disorder when she was younger too. I knew her back then and I was able to see the things she went through. She went to an eating disorder clinic in Utah, I believe it was. She spent a year there and then after that is when we got together. So I knew recovery was possible. I'd seen it. I was determined—it didn't matter what—I was determined that my daughter was going to get better. It gave me hope, for sure it did.

I was very fortunate to understand it already, because so many people don't understand it. I remember people saying, "Well, just make her eat. It will be okay." Thanks a lot! You have no idea! There's so many people, you can explain it to them, you can sit down and talk to them for six hours, and they still don't understand it. They say they do, but they don't. They need to walk through that Unit, to see these poor people, how sick they are, the trauma those poor girls have gone through. Who knows what's gone on in their lives. [The eating disorder] is their outlet. That's there way of control, of coping. I can't imagine sitting there and thinking, 'Do I eat this or do I not eat this?' That's what goes through their minds.

- **What have you learned?**

I know that I'm a very caring and loving person. I've realized how strong I am. Now I'm reaching out and I'm trying to help other people through things. My cousin is going to Henwood [Treatment Center] on Monday for an alcohol addiction. Just being there for him—we don't talk about it [the addiction]—just phoning him, showing up, showing him that I care. That's a gift that I'm giving back too. With my cousin being as sick as he is, I've said to my other brother, "Phone him, he needs you." And he says, "What do you mean he needs me?" "Just phone him, let him know you are there." But some people just don't get it. You have to experience it. You have to have gone through something in your life, so you are able to give back.

- **Recovery**

Recovery would be, she's doing well, she's eating properly, she's taking care of herself properly, keeping it in check. It's all those things but it's also her knowing that she's aware of it, because it doesn't go away. It doesn't end. It's always there. I've seen that with my ex-wife: she went backwards.

There were a few times where Cassie was starting to falter; she was struggling. I'd say to Cassie, "OK. Cassie, I'm making you an appointment." "Dad, I don't want to." "Cassie, we need to."

Dr. O has been amazing. She was excellent. I would email her at 7, 8, 9 o'clock at night and she'd fire back an email at 11 o'clock at night with an update on Cassie. Cassie had a very hard time with Dr. P, they did not hit it off, they clashed. She trashed his office and then went running out and they locked the place down. They went into lockdown! She was only X lbs, but she was so violent and so aggressive. I don't know what it was, but they clashed and we didn't know what we were going to do. We thought, "Oh no, now what?" And then we found out Dr. O had an opening and we went in there immediately, saw Dr. O and Cassie connected with her. I think that connection was what really, really helped. Dr. O gives so much to this program. I wish there were more people like her. It's so demanding on her. Dr. O: I just can't say enough good about her.

Recovery was everything all put together. Counselling sessions. Cassie starting to get a better understanding of herself. It was even the schooling. She did all her schooling there {Stollery school] and she excelled at it. It gave her a boost to start believing in herself. I can't pin it on one thing.

It's such a big, big thing [eating disorders] and there's not enough treatment for it. There needs to be more, I honestly think so, but I don't know if there are enough qualified people to do it. You have to be very special to do it. The whole hospital—right from the Stollery then going over to that Unit, the nurses themselves, everyone in that ward—they give a lot more than just their job.

They gave us information on where we can stay. It's scary coming from smaller centers, you just don't know. At first, we were staying in hotels. Of course, you can't afford that. So to go to *Ronald McDonald House* and to stay there for 20-some dollars a night, it was amazing. Even when we weren't staying in Edmonton at night, *Ronald McDonald House* would open its doors to us and let us come visit for the day and go to the games room. We'd just hang out there. It was nice.

• Life now

My relationship with my daughter is amazing now. There's a lot more communication with my daughter, we talk a lot more now, there's more trust. We've grown so much closer. Spending time with her and getting to know her better. With my other daughter too.

It's a long journey; it hasn't ended. Myself, I'm still on edge because I'm still worrried. I have to let that go, not being on her all the time. "Are you eating? Are you eating?" Because it seems the more an adult does that, the more it drives them into it. You need to know when to ease up and just watch. That's all you can do. That's what I've had to learn through this too: Step back. Let her do it. Not: "I'll carry you." I have to let her walk.

Cassie is very mature; she's an amazing girl. She's very self-aware. I look at what she's been through, what a beautiful person, how strong she is. She's not scared to say what she believes, her point of view. She stands up for herself. She's got a mind of her own. That alone. They do become stronger.

And now she's talking about going to college. ("I don't want you to go! I want you to stay here with Dad!") Of course, you want the best for your daughter; you want everything to go perfectly, but you know they have to grow up, make their own mistakes... just like we did. She may not understand it or see it, but down the road, she will look back and go, "Wow! Look at what they did for me."

RESEARCH SAYS

Studies done at the University of California School of Medicine (San Diego) have found that people who suffer from anorexia often have common personality traits, which were present long before the eating disorder manifests. These traits include:

- anxiety/depression
- perfectionism
- people-pleasing
- obsessiveness with symmetry and exactness
- struggles with uncertainty, worrying about future, criticizing past thoughts
- rule abiding, rigid, harm avoidance

TO LEARN MORE

http://eatingdisorders.ucsd.edu/research/biocorrelates/PDFs/Kaye2010NeurobiologyofAN.pdf

The Starvation Study

One of the things I found most useful was reading about a study that was done in 1944 by Ancel Keys and his colleagues at the University of Minnesota. It's commonly referred to as The Starvation Study. The experiment involved 36 men, who were chosen for the study because they were extremely fit, both physically and mentally. They were asked to restrict their diet to half their normal caloric intake and, over six months, they lost on average about 25% of their body weight. After six months, they were restored to their previous weight and throughout the experiment they were monitored for effects and behaviour.

None of these men had eating disorders before the experiment, but all of them demonstrated eating disordered behaviours during the starvation experiment. They became obsessed with food conversations, began collecting utensils and cookbooks and chewed gum obsessively. Some began to sneak food and binge uncontrollably; some vomited and were filled with self-reproach. Their mood and dispositions changed remarkably. They were irritable or prone to outbursts of anger. Some felt apathetic, withdrawn, depressed, anxious and some began ignoring their personal hygiene. They isolated themselves and felt socially inadequate. Some began self-mutilating—one man even cut off three of his fingers! Their concentration, alertness, comprehension and judgement were all impacted. They had poor circulation, visual disturbances, hair loss, dizziness, headaches, lower heart rates and lower metabolic rates.

As I read this list of symptoms, I mentally ticked off all the things that Hannah was experiencing. It helped me to understand the effects of starvation. I shared the article to help explain her behaviours to other people: "This is what the brain does when it doesn't have enough food. Food is her medicine. These symptoms won't go away until her weight is restored."

TO LEARN MORE

http://en.wikipedia.org/wiki/Minnesota_Starvation_Experiment

http://www.psychologytoday.com/blog/hunger-artist/201011/starvation-study-shows-recovery-anorexia-is-possible-only-regaining-weight

PHOTO: EILEEN SPROULE

Julia

Julia was 26 years old at the time of the interview.
Her eating disorder manifested when she was 16.

"It started innocently. It all came together like a perfect storm."

"I remember writing down the communion wafer I'd had at church.
You count that!"

• Summary

Julia: It started in Grade 10/Grade 11. I never had a boyfriend, so my idea for getting a boyfriend was to shed some of this weight, start taking better care of my appearance, stop being the tomboy, become more of a woman. I was active with piano, dancing, the different bands in school, other social clubs, Student Council. I got busy. It was just go, go, go; I didn't have time to snack in front of the TV for hours in the evening. For me, it all started innocently. It all came together... like a perfect storm.

The big crunch came Grade 12: I just kept losing the weight and I actually strove to lose the weight. I remember trying on my grad dress. I got it March 1st and it fit quite well and then when I went to try it on again down the road, I'd lost even more weight. I remember my Mom saying, "You just wanted to fit in that stupid dress" and so she blamed it on the dress.

And then that summer, it was a big transition for me going from Grade 12: coming from a graduating class of 55 in a small rural town to university in the big city; being independent; living on my own. It scared me because I'd always been protected by Mom and Dad.

(*Julia brings out a photo album and begins looking at photos*) I look at the pictures from that summer and I see how I looked and it scares me. That was a bad summer. I lost all my muscle mass. I didn't see it at the time, but I definitely see it now. It happened so long ago. It's difficult to remember. My brain was nothing. All I have is these photos. I don't remember.

I was working in a store from grade 9 to 12 and the owner told my mom, "Hey, I think your daughter has an eating disorder," because her daughter had an eating disorder. She recommended that we go see Dr. O and I thought Mom was nuts. "Are you kidding? I'm not sick." She even started weighing me. *Effff!!* I'm not going to go see someone! I'm fine! I ate three meals a day: breakfast had to be at 6, lunch had to be at noon, supper had to be at 6. I didn't vomit. I just restricted what I ate and pushed myself.

But that January, 2006, I had a chat with Dr. O. We basically talked about me. And then she brought in Mom and Dad and chatted with them. And then we all sat down, the four of us, and she said, "This is Julia and she has anorexia, the restrictive type" and I honestly laughed at her: "You're kidding, right? I don't have an eating disorder." The laughing—was it a shield? To deflect? To deny? I'm very defiant. Stubborn and set in my ways. I liked the routine and I didn't want to change it.

And they took me for an ECG and some blood work and I was concerned: "I'm missing school. Mom and Dad, you're paying for me to be in school and I'm at some silly appointment. This is ridiculous!"

(*Julia brings out a journal from that time*)
I was so paranoid, I kept a journal of everything I ate. At the very beginning, I even remember writing down the communion wafer I'd have at church— "You count that Dr. O!" My gosh, that's how obsessive I was.

I haven't read this in a while. My gosh. My first entry. (*reading*) "Thursday January 12, 2006. For lunch, I had a whole wheat pita." I only ate half. "3 leafs of lettuce, 4 cucumbers, one mushroom, 2 fingers of oven roasted chicken. ½ cup of fruit cocktail." I even added in the gum. That is beyond necessary. (*finding another page*) There it is: "Communion wafer, red wine". I wanted that to be counted. (*laughs*)

As the year progressed, I kept seeing Dr. O, going for appointments two times a week, but I kept losing weight. I thought of it, initially, as a game. Dr. O would have me take off my shoes (to get weighed) and she'd say, "Oh! You are wearing a heavy belt or heavy sweater, take that off before I weigh you." Some days I'd go in thinking: 'I haven't taken a poop today!' That was my little jab at her. I was working against her initially; I didn't see her value. I'd get angry at her a lot, yell at her and say, "I feel sorry for your kids because you work here all the time." I was angry with her and the world. I did not like her. Now, I'm very thankful for what she offered... the shit I put her through!

I went for meals for a week on the Unit because my brother wasn't home. I told Dr O that and I started mentioning some of the girls' names. She didn't like the fact that I was associating myself with other girls with eating disorders. If you put all these people with ED in one room, they kind of egg each other on. The atmosphere can be good on the Unit, but it can be bad, too. Especially if some aren't ready to get better.

I remember walking on the Unit and looking at other girls: 'Why is she skinnier than me? I want to look like that.' I was constantly comparing myself with every single one of them. 'They didn't get milk on their dinner tray, why did I get milk?' It may not be the best way towards healing, but how else can you go about it?

It was that summer, the summer of 2006, my older sister and I were driving back to Edmonton after a weekend at the farm and she broke down crying in the car with me. It was on Highway 16, right at Ukrainian Village, and she just shattered. She said, "You're not getting better! Why?" I said, "I'm trying." She said, "Well, try harder!" I could hear she was really upset. I could hear that in her voice. I could see she was frustrated and angry with me. And that got me upset. So I asked her, "What do you want from me?" And she wiped her eyes and said, "I want you to be happy."

So deep down I knew what I wanted: I wanted for them to be happy. I still remember where we were: there was no snow on the shoulders of the road, it was clouded over. I remember it like it was yesterday. That was a very pinnacle moment. So from then on, I kept asking Dr. O for different strategies, what to eat...and so it began.

I have always knocked heads with my sister. She was always independent, doing her own thing, but she would write me letters. I remember one—it was a big sign that said: "I believe in you." And I put that up on the wall and it helped push me through.

• Turning points

I remember Mom and Dad were going to a funeral and they asked, "Would you like to come?" and I said, "Sure." And I remember pacing in the living room, and they said, "Would you have a seat?" and I said, "No, I can't sit down, I have to stand." Because, of course, standing burns more calories. I said, "I realize I'm sick. I know I'll get better, but this is just what I have to do." That was a turning point, allowing Mom and Dad to see me.

I never told many people about this... but this was in my recovery stage (from restricting), when I was bingeing a lot, just eating anything I could get my hands on. I would count out my pennies, nickels and dimes and go to the store to see how much candy I could buy. I would eat cups and cups of candies at night. I would go through phases of eating bags of marshmallows or chocolate chips. I don't know if I craved the sugar or what it was. One day, I came home from church and I was ravenous. I made a 9 by 9 cake and I ate three quarters of it and I was feeling really poopy. So I went for a long walk down 142nd Street and all of a sudden my stomach started rumbling. Oh *shit!* I need to go to the bathroom...I didn't make it.

It was awful; it was an awful feeling. I'm 20 years old and I shit my pants. It was horrible. This is not the lifestyle I want for me! I don't want to be this person. At that moment, it was like I put down this mental fist down in my mind: 'This has to stop!!'

• Recovery

It's not easy. It's not a short road; it won't happen overnight. Even now, seven years after diagnosis, I'm still on the road to recovery. I still don't think I'm fully recovered. I still have restrictions. To this day, I still haven't had a glass of *Pepsi*. I still haven't eaten potato chips or a french fry at *Wendy's*. But this year was big: I started eating corn chips!

Sue: I'm not sure you need to eat exactly like everyone else to be considered "recovered." If you never eat another french fry in your life, is that important?

Julia: A normal person would be able to have things in moderation.

Sue: I guess if you feel limited by not having a french fry, if it bothers you, then you can keep working towards that. [NOTE: *Since this interview, Julia has added french fries and potato chips to her food repertoire.*]

Julia: I may be discharged from the program, but I'm still fighting the battles. [They] may not be daily, may not be weekly, but it may be on a monthly basis. I know it's hard to be discouraged over and over again. It's a long tunnel but there is a light at the end. The light was very, very small to begin with and now it's getting quite a bit bigger.

• The gift

What have I learned from this? You can control the condition. Initially, I was definitely letting it control me. Some people have a name for their eating disorder, they call it *Timmy* or *Ed* or whatever. Mine was just *The Thing* or *It* and *It* definitely controlled me and then there was a turning point: I was beginning to control *It*. The other thing I've learned is to be more accepting of people with mental illness. If I see someone who is a psych patient, I think, 'They are human. They have problems, big whoop.' It's helped me be more accepting... because I'm one of them.

My family, I've always known we are very connected, very supportive of each other. I think I realize now even more what I put them through during that time period. One evening, my parents couldn't get hold of us, they packed up the car, and drove into town to find us sleeping upstairs. We just didn't hear the phone. That showed that they really cared, that they'd get in the car and drive, for an hour and a half, in the middle of the night, in winter. They just dropped everything to come.

Another evening I went out with some friends to a bar on Jasper Ave. We're out dancing, but I don't feel good. I go to the bar and kind of put my head down on a stool and the bartender comes over, "Hey are you okay?" And then before I know it, I'm on the floor, looking up, I don't know what's going on. Nothing makes sense, I just hear voices. Someone grapples me up in their arms and take me to the back then they are shoving some orange juice and crackers in my face. I don't want that! That's the last thing I want!

And the Emergency Response Team comes in and they take one look at my collarbone, "Oh gosh, look at her" and so I tell them I have an eating disorder. They take me to the Misericordia Hospital. And they are trying to get hold of my brother and my heart rate is going so low that the monitor is beeping. "Oh gosh, she's coding on us." And I'm like: 'I'm still alive. What's the big deal?' My brother is jumping up every time it beeps and I'm laughing at him. Like it was a joke.

It's not until I look back with healthy eyes that I can see it: "Wow, I was really sick." I remember Dad told me, later, I could have been six feet under ground. I know now, for how sick I was, it was a miracle I wasn't.

- **Emotions**

I was scared. There was a lot of fear: I can't go out, I can't eat out, I have to know what I'm eating. I couldn't for the life of me stay and eat with the family. Only trusted people could cook for me. I trusted my brother, who lived with me. I think, truthfully, he was scared of me, so he just did what I requested of him. I rarely went home at this time period and I think that even worried Mom and Dad more.

- **How did you overcome the setbacks and keep going?**

I think the thing that really saved me was to have my goal in my cross arrows and to see it: I'm going to get a degree. My motivation was 'Eat so you can go to school.' So that's how I got through my first year of university: Eating so I can go to school. And then, of course, seeing the benefits from eating: getting these marks back and thinking, "Wow! How did I get these marks?" Of course: feed your brain and things happen. My memory was amazing. I think just being loved helped. I haven't found my love until recently. Having other people find me attractive. I know that sounds shallow. I'm definitely aware it sounds awful.

Sue: I think we all need to feel loved, to feel loveable. That's not shallow. It's a human need. Being defined solely by how other people see us, being convinced that only the exterior matters, maybe that's shallow.

Julia: When I was at my skinniest weight, I met this guy at the bar and he tried to pick me up. So, a few days later, I met up with him to watch the game and I think him seeing me when he was sober, seeing how sick I looked... I never heard boo from him again.

I always equated it this way: I need to be skinny to get a man who loves me. But that's not how it goes, of course. At my lowest weight, no one could love me... versus where I am now, my happy medium.

• Hope

Initially, I just thought I was going to be like that forever. But with little tidbits from Dr. O, saying, "Hey, try eating granola or try eating nut mix to nudge in the calories" comes a bit of weight gain and you get a clearer sense of thinking. You need some brain cells to realize what's going on and to have hope.

Sue: That makes so much sense because hope is really about the future. In order to think about the future, the frontal cortex of the brain needs to be functioning. So until the brain is nourished, it's pretty hard to conceptualize hope.

• Life now

Life is peachy. I'm looking forward to the future. I'm turning 26 in a few days. I'm looking forward to someday being a wife, having kids, excelling in my career. I'm looking at the big picture. It's not what I'm going to eat for my next meal. I still have battles. Some days I go out to the corner market for candies and eat the whole bag. And then I feel like crap, but I tell myself, 'Tomorrow's another day.' Just start over and try to power through difficult times. Having a good support network is key.

My boyfriend helped me get my confidence back. A lot of it was being loved—not just by my family—for who I am. He loves me the way I am. He doesn't care if I have a little extra here or there. It's the best feeling ever. I haven't felt this great in my skin, ever. The future looks good.

• Staying well

It comes down to the balance, you eat healthy, you work out well, not rigorously or anything... when you have a balance of everything in your life, you will stay healthy. A little bit of fun, a little bit of focus. It's a 24/7 devotion to trying to get better.

• One sentence

I wouldn't wish it upon my worst enemy. It's an awful thing to go through. I wouldn't want to go through it again. Maybe that's my fear of having a daughter (or even a son, I'm not saying it can't happen to males.) Is it genetic? Will my kids have an eating disorder?

• Have I missed anything?

Initially, the big hurdle was Dr. O wanted to throw me on some meds. I was like, "I don't want meds. That will change my whole personality." But (*laughs*) I didn't have a personality anyway!! Did it really matter?! Eventually, I took the meds. It was after I freaked out. There's no other way of explaining it. I shook and screamed and grabbed my hair in front of my brother. He started crying. It scared him. That was another turning point. I thought: 'I gotta stop hurting people I care about.'

I remember I was trying all these different meds. My pharmacist made a very nice analogy for me, he said, "Imagine your medicine is like a toolbox. We're trying the screwdriver, we're trying the hammer. We just need to find the right tool that will work for you, for your case."

Sue: I like that. There is a lot of stigma around taking medication for mental illness. It helps to think about the meds as a tool.

Julia: The day I come off them [the meds], totally, I'm scared for that day. What will happen? I have tried to come off them and I lost all control. I couldn't focus. Maybe one day. Does that define being healed?

Sue: Well, what about a diabetic? They take insulin forever. Does anyone judge them for that?

Julia: Yeah, you're right.

"Encouraging patients to gain weight asks them to do the very thing of which they are most frightened. Patients may believe that the psychiatrist just wants to make them fat and does not understand or empathize with their underlying emotions."

— *Practice Guideline for the Treatment of Patients with Eating Disorders* Third Edition, American Psychiatric Association, 2006

PHOTO: JENNY HAWKINS

Helen (Julia's mom)

"I promised her that we would not talk about it and I never have. This is giving me my voice."

"If you could take it away and you could bear it for them, you would do it as a parent. But you can't."

Sue: Why did you agree to participate in this book?

(*long pause*)

Helen: I can't sit and do this. I need to *stand*... (*stands up, moves, pause, emotion rising*)... I can't...

(*I turn off the microphone off, we pause, when she's ready I hit record again*)

Helen: (*pause*) ...it is a continuation of the support for Julia. That's it. Even though it's hard. Julia has been very "This is My Story." Like she said, "Don't you dare talk to anyone at work about this." She didn't want to be the topic of discussion. And I promised her that we would not talk about it and I never have.

Sue: That's a lot for you to carry, for a very long time.

Helen: And maybe this is giving me my voice? I did not think I would be this emotional. I really didn't.

But this goes back to Day One when I did not know Julia had an eating disorder. It was in Grade 12 and the school counsellor had phoned me and said, "Well, Julia fainted." We had talked about it—why—and she said well she just got light-headed and all that sort of stuff. I didn't put two and two together, yet. The school counsellor had phoned and said, "Julia has an eating disorder." No, you're full of it, because Julia eats a very good breakfast and she eats a very good supper. So I said, "She doesn't have an eating disorder." But I said, "Thank you for letting me know. I will keep watching."

A few months later, two other people in our community came up to me. One person pulled me into the back of his store and said he thinks Julia has an eating disorder. And I says, "Thank you again." I says, "You're not the first person to say that and I'm keeping an eye and I'm just watching." The third person came to our house and said Julia has an eating disorder. I said, "Thank you, we're looking into it"...blah, blah, blah.

But the seed was planted. After that, if I would put my hand on her back or shoulder, when she was working at the computer, I noticed the shrugs started. You know, like, "Don't touch me." And I could feel her backbone.

So, I phoned my doctor. Then I phoned the Eating Disorder Clinic in Edmonton to set up the initial appointment. As soon as I hung up the phone, I burst out crying, because I felt that I was turning my daughter in. And then when Julia had her first appointment with Dr. Ostolosky, because she was over the age of 18, my husband and I were asked to leave the room. And they said, "Come back in an hour." And so when we did, Julia had told Dr. Ostolosky, "Just watch, Mom's going to start crying." (*laughs, taking out a Kleenex*) So you know, this is full circle. And I'll just have you pause it again, so you don't hear the honking. (*laughs. I turn off the microphone for a moment*)

Helen: In our circle of friends, they know little bits and parts, but I kept that promise to Julia so she wouldn't become... you know, small town living....

Sue: The topic of gossip?

Helen: You got it. You got it.

Sue: That must have been a very difficult promise to keep. Did you have other people you were able to talk to?

Helen: In the family itself, we would talk about it. Mom would be my sounding board. I would talk to her or my sister. My boss and the secretary knew, so if Dr. Ostolosky ever phoned me at work—and she did—they knew to immediately put the phone through to me, even if I was in the middle of a meeting or whatever. The secretary would bring me the cordless phone and I'd be pacing the halls, just talking it through with Dr. Ostolosky when there were some issues that had come up. She would talk to me. So that was good too, being able to talk to her too. Maybe that's what I needed.

There was so much I didn't know. I only thought there was one kind of purging. I was so mistaken. I did not know there was such a thing as an exercise purge and that was what Julia was doing. Unless she's told you different? Because I never thought that she'd be purging in the house. It was always when she would go off for her long walks, and that's when she would be doing her exercising. Because a nutritious breakfast? Portion-controlled sizes? She did all that.

Sue: Yes, and being so fit and active, you think 'my kid's doing great.'

Helen: Oh yes, playing soccer. President of the Student Union. She was one of the Mistress of Ceremonies for the grad exercises...

• How would you describe the journey?

An emotional roller coaster. Julia would vent a lot of her—I don't know if rage is the best word—she would vent to me. And because of the distance—she was here in Edmonton, we were out at the farm—it was never face-to-face. I think maybe that would have be different. But because she would use the phone, she would be venting rather loudly and emotionally. I would have to... it took a lot of self-control not to retaliate. I could not take it personally. I think that was the main thing was not to take it personally. Especially when my husband would get on the phone with her and she would be all nicey-nicey-nicey. (*laughs*) He never saw it. I'd say, "Julia was very angry and talking about this and that." He'd say, "Oh no."

She was talking about other things to him. I was her target. If I needed to be—well, I suppose that's being a sacrificing mother, in order to help with her recovery, so be it.

Why did I get her anger? Because I turned her in! (*laughs*) Probably because I'm the one that the kids come to if they have a problem. They come to me and I'd be the one to be talking to them, guiding them through the process. I don't know. That would be a good question for Julia. They go to one parent for certain things and then they know they go to the other parent for other things. So I became that parent.

Sue: Lucky you!

Helen: (*laughs*) Yeah.

Sue: What were the hardest parts for you?

Helen: Obviously, the secrecy! (*laughs*) Just holding it in. (*pause*) That it wasn't anything that I did. Not to blame myself for Julia's choices. I'm still searching for the reason why. We live on a farm, we always have home-grown carrots, and always eating healthy. Why? I still don't know whether it was the magazines, was it something someone said? I wonder if it wasn't envy towards some of her other classmates that were in size zero clothes. I looked at Julia and I said, "You are big boned. You are not going to be a size zero." (*responding, as Julia:*) "Why not??? I want to be!!!" Don't they realize what they're doing to themselves?

- **Were there any turning points?**

Back in our home town, she danced for ten, twelve years. The instructor has a group here in Edmonton and she went to start dancing with them. She happened to tell her doctor and her doctor said, "No. No way are you dancing." Because at that time, with her blood work, her heart, dance was going to be too strenuous. And Julia listened to her. And I thought, 'Oh! Maybe we've have been too permissive as parents.' Always supporting the kids, whatever they would do. "If you chose to do that, 'kay, we'll be behind you. We'll support you" and for her doctor to say, "Hey! No!" That was one turning point, then the other one was going to the clinic. That was an eye-opening experience.

There were little bits and pieces that helped Julia take charge of her own life. She did it herself.

- **How would you define recovery?**

Recovery is being able to acknowledge the fact that you do have an eating disorder and to be able to take charge of your life. Not let that eating disorder take charge of you.

I don't think it's finished—that's my view—because, even a few months ago, she said, "Mom, it's been ten years since I walked into a *McDonalds*." And it's like a badge of honour for her. I was thinking why would that be so important to her? And then again it's the self-blame afterwards. I'm thinking: 'Is it because when we were leaving Edmonton to go back home, we'd stop at *McDonalds*?' So was that why? Because she was in *McDonalds*—I didn't think it was that often—is that why? I don't know. I still go back to that: if she can still say that and be so proud, there must be still something niggling at the back.

- **What has this experience give you?**

That's a hard question.

The perseverance to endure something like this as a family. And it hasn't broken us up. The fact it has, in some ways, brought us together more. We can rise above it. We can still be a family. We still get along.

- **Has it taught you anything about yourself?**

That I could be so patient? (*laughs*). I suppose that there's no such thing as the perfect family also. We have four kids. They've all gone to post-secondary and you're thinking everything is going fine. Nobody has gone into drugs. How can this come into your family? I know there has been some shifting of family dynamics between Julia and her elder sister, Tanya. Julia has been very angry because Tanya also has lost weight. She's ranted at me, "Why don't you get after Tanya like you did me?" I didn't realize some of the things her brother, John, has seen also. He never came home and talked about it. He's kept it in also. He has to be a male. He hasn't talked about it. I did phone him. I left a message on his cellphone, "Sue Huff is coming to the condo, 4 o'clock, if you have time..." I had mentioned to Katrin [her younger sister] she could come say something as well. (*Both chose not to participate.*)

Katrin told me she was here when you had that interview with Julia and there were some things that Julia told you and Katrin had told me. And I thought, 'Pardon me? WHAT?!' I did not realise Julia thought it was a game. "It was just a game." Pardon me? When she faints and was basically in a coma for a couple of hours because her heart was under 24 (beats a minute). That was a game to you?! This was life and death. I'm thinking in my brain, 'How could someone so intelligent be so stupid?'

When Julia was at university in her first year, she ended up fainting and was unconscious. A few days later, I'm trying to get hold of her. I'm phoning and there's no answer on the phone. And no answer. We had given her a cellphone and she, in her stubbornness... maybe that was the problem: we gave it to her... anyway, she wouldn't put it on. At midnight, I'm phoning. I'm phoning the U of A and the Misericordia and the Royal Alex. Where's Julia?! At midnight, we bundled up Katrin and we drove into Edmonton to find Julia. I did not know the phone was out of whack here at the condo. Yeah, she was here. So we just got a hotel room and went back home the next morning.

• Isolation

I know there are other people in our home town who have kids with eating disorders. Did I seek them out to talk to them? No. Is there a support group for the parents? No. Maybe that's what there should be: a support group for the parents too because you are going through this. Or even family counselling. As a family, you are all going through this. And then also there is that stigma that is with any mental illness.

My mother-in-law, she's in her mid-eighties, she did not believe it. She says, "No she doesn't have an eating disorder; she eats. What does that mean?" And with my sister-in-law, it would have been: "We won't talk about it. It's a private family matter. No, we're not going to talk about it." People just float away.

• Hope

I had hope for Julia that she would, with her doctor, with her family love and with support, that she could overcome it. There had to be hope, otherwise, oh, it would have been so... If there wasn't hope for us that yes, she could get better... Oh, it would have been useless. I don't know... Would there *be* a recovery then? But because there is hope, that yes, you can get better then that keeps you going, just like the *Energizer Bunny*. You just keep on going and keep on going. And allowing her to vent. And it's baby steps. Sometimes the baby steps are going forward and sometimes it's a couple back, but you know you're going to go forward again.

Seeing those little baby steps gave me hope. That Julia took the cards—those healthy eating cards that her doctor gave her—and she said, "Yup, I followed them today" and I go: 'YES! Bonus! She did it!' She would start eating some food that was listed as taboo before. 'YES!' Just those little victories. It wouldn't be something I would be jumping up and down and going "*Woohoo!*" in front of Julia because I don't know if Julia would have appreciated that. I don't think she would have. So I would just say, "Good. I'm glad you're eating that." Give her the support. Give her the big hug and such, but on the inside, I'd be jumping up and down. She had broken another one of those hurdles or those taboos she had set up for herself and she was able to do it.

Sue: It's almost like they build themselves a prison of rules.

Helen: Yes, there were so many rules: I can't do this. I can't do that. I have to do the twenty lunges or whatever.

A definition of hope is that there is a better life than what they are living right now. The hope is that they'll get better and recover. And stay there. *And stay there.*

If there were to be a relapse, I would think it would be if there's... um... an emotional time for Julia. I'm thinking that if her and her boyfriend break up, then I think there would be a relapse. So we just watch for the signs and try to be the support for the kids, like we've always been or tried to be.

- **Life now**

Life now is not like it was seven years ago. She has completed some of her life goals. I don't have to sit there and worry about her. I don't have to go to bed at night worrying, 'Where's Julia?' You know how there was always the worry? When you wake up in the morning and think, 'Oh, what is she going to eat today?'

You try not to hover, but show support. You don't want to be watching them while they're eating, with hawk eyes, because then they won't be themselves. They may take to hiding things and all that. That was something we had to work through.

- **Key to staying well**

For her, I think just to be able to look at that black cloud—if it's still there, I hope it's really, really small—but be able to look at that black cloud and shrug it off. And say: "I am more than that. I can continue to do what I want in my life without having that black cloud following me." What is that Charlie Brown character? Pigpen! With that big cloud of dust all the time! Not to have that cloud behind you all the time. Just to go out and enjoy her life. Not to worry about what she looks like, when she looks in the mirror.

Sorry for the tears. (*laughs*)

I'm thinking about someone who had lived with a man who had an alcohol problem—this was thirty years ago—and she said, "Living with an alcoholic, every day is a brand new day. You shrug off what he said the day before and you start every day as a brand new day." That's basically the same with an eating disorder—whatever happened the day before, whatever the phone call was—the next time I phone her, it's (*brightly*) "Hi! How are you doing today?" And not harbour any griefs or ill feelings. Don't take it personally. Just one day at a time.

Sue: I think one of the challenges for me is letting go of deadlines. I'm so fixated on time lines, that the open-endedness of this journey to recovery is hard for me. I just wish I knew how long it was going to take and when we would "get there."

Helen: We cannot take their eating disorder away from them. It's something they have to work through for themselves, by themselves. If you could take it away and you could bear it for them, you would do it, as a mother. But you can't. It's something they have to do for themselves.

Sue: Yes, I've wanted to rip it away, yank it away! But they hold on tighter if you pull. So I have to let go. And let her take the steps when she is ready to take them.

Helen: I know people at church, they ask, "How is Julia. Is she recovered?" So I give that hesitant reply: "Well, she's eating. She's got her weight back. She's doing everything she loves." I suppose that's the thing: she's happy.

It's interesting, Julia is now at a point that she is able to be more open about the eating disorder. I thought it started in Grade 12 and she said, "No, it was in Grade 10."

Crying

Several months into the journey, our daughter blurted out: "Why am I the only one crying?"

I said, "Oh, honey. I cry all the time, you just don't see it."

"Why not?" she asked.

"I thought it would just add to your burden. But if you want to see me cry, no problem. The tears are always just there below the surface... seconds away."

"It would help me to not feel like such a freak."

So we went home, cuddled up on the couch, wrapped ourselves in a blanket and bawled.

PHOTO: EILEEN SPROULE

Olivia

First sign: Grade 3
Illness emerged: Grade 9
Age at interview: 17 years old (Grade 12)
Wait for treatment after diagnosis: 10 months
Treated as outpatient (ongoing): 1 year

"The biggest thing is feeling really fragile, if someone touched me, I could break."

"People with eating disorders feel that what's inside them isn't worth being loved."

• Overview of your story

Olivia: I don't remember ever really being normal about food. I was a little bit heavier and I got made fun of quite a bit for it and that obviously sucks, but I didn't consciously do anything to change it until spring break of Grade 3. I remember my parents taking me and my brother out to *Swiss Chalet* for this big treat and my parents were like "What do you want?" and I was like, "Nothing!!" I just screamed and I know myparents were embarrassed, but I just screamed I didn't want anything! I ran upstairs. I was gagging at the smell of food. They tried to get me to eat one fry and I couldn't. I couldn't even look at food without feeling nauseous. That lasted for all of spring break and I think I lost "X" pounds in four days.

They took me to the hospital, I got admitted and I got all my blood work done, IVs put in. I was there for probably eight hours with my dad. They were just like, "She just needs to eat." We came home. I don't know if it scared me, being in the hospital, but all of a sudden a switch went off, and they gave me *Cheerios* and I remember sitting with my brother, watching TV, and it was fine. I think that's where my main issue with food started. Ever since then, I've just been really weird with it. There are times when I will just eat and eat and eat or just won't eat.

My whole life has revolved around food. [As a kid] I was chubbier and I got tested for diabetes. I got tested for all these things. My doctor told my parents to take me to a dietician. I was weighed. I was told what to eat, when to eat. My family, because I was bigger, was always saying things. And when I did lose weight, it was a big congratulations. My whole life has been so consumed with it. I see myself getting better, but I see my life always circling around it. So, I'm not there yet. Recovery to me, for myself, would be thinking about food in a normal way. Or eating and feeling okay about it. That's when I will know I'm better.

The bulimia started in Grade 9. I thought it was another way to fix things, right? Often I get obsessed with something for a really short period of time, and then I just don't think about it. So I can not eat for a while, because I get obsessed with not eating, but it won't last. But this [bulimia] stuck. I'm still struggling with it. So that's Grade 9 to Grade 12... three years.

Battling myself, mostly, has been the biggest obstacle. It's was like a constant war of *Not Wanting To Do It* and *Wanting To*. You constantly have that, where I so badly want to go throw up, but like I'm ashamed of myself. 'No Olivia, you don't actually want to do that.' So, it's just a constant battle. I get better, haven't done it and then I have a day where this part takes over and all of sudden there I am, in the bathroom and I'm like, 'How does this happen?'

Sue: How do you overcome that urge?

Olivia: Being distracted, trying to distract myself.

Sue: What kinds of things do you use to distract yourself?

Olivia: Just thinking about anything. Sitting down watching TV. I have to distract myself for a certain amount of time... Half an hour probably.

• Who has helped you over the past three years?

In Grade 10, I met this guy, and we dated for a year and a half and he was my best friend, and he was the only one, besides my parents, who knew. He helped me through it, so much. Also my parents, my family just being behind me. I want to say all these people helped, but personally I feel like I'm the one who's helped me the most. No one can fix it for me. So if I've gotten any better, it's because I've wanted to, I think.

There have been lots of little turning points. I think one of the biggest one was—that guy in Grade 10—me and him not really talking anymore, him kind of moving on. That was really hard for me, because I did lean on him a lot, so that was really hard to have one of those supports gone. I had to re-adjust everything. That was a big turning point for me: learning that if someone is gone, you just can't collapse. I had to pick myself back up. I'm really glad that he stopped supporting me, so I could learn how to be more self-sufficient.

A few months into my treatment—so in Grade 10—my therapist was like, "You know what? You don't need to come here anymore 'cuz you're not putting in any effort. I don't see any change. I don't see you wanting anything." I just bawled for a day. Just cried. And then I was like, "She's right. Why am I wasting her time, if I'm not going to get better?" That's really big: for people to call you out. As much as it's going to hurt you—and I'm sure she didn't like to see me, literally shaking, crying so bad, in the hospital—but you can't just baby us either. As babyish as we are and as babied as I'd like to be, it's not going to help. Hold us accountable. My parents said, "Are you okay seeing this therapist?" and I said, "Yes." If I say I'm okay to go see her, I have to be ready to make changes.

At the beginning, my parents were really closely monitoring me and I'm really glad now they have kind of let me try and figure it out on my own. I think when they started to do that, it was huge, because I was then, 'OK, it's up to me now whether I want to get better or I don't.' I think that was a big turning point.

To me, it [bulimia] is like a comfort. It's a comfort thing. And I feel very vulnerable without it. I also feel very vulnerable talking about it and very vulnerable being in an area where they want to know about it, because it's such a secret part of you that to completely give it to your doctor and go, "Okay, make me better" is the hardest thing to do. It's so hard to be open with people about it. It's taken me a really long time to be open about it. And I'm still obviously not going to be open about everything, but you really just have to open yourself up. You feel really vulnerable. Extremely vulnerable.

Sue: So, every time I'm asking my daughter to tell me about her eating disorder, it's like asking her to strip naked in front of me?

Olivia: Except way worse.

Sue: Why is it worse?

Olivia: It's not just what you see, it's everything inside that you've been carrying around. And you have to let go of all that too: what caused it, why you are still holding on, angers you have at people that made you do it. Like I have to let go of all of the people who made fun of me when I was younger. I have to forgive my doctor my making my parents take me to a dietician. I have to forgive my parents for taking to me to a dietician when I was eight. There's all those things and I'm still constantly forgiving people. Some people will say little things that are upsetting, I have to be like, "OK, they don't realize." I remember one time at dance, one of my really good friends—and I never talked to her about which I probably should have—we were talking, and she was saying, "If I could, I would throw up this food, but I don't want to because it's disgusting." That was really rotten. That was really hard. You constantly have to forgive other people and yourself. And I think that's why it's so hard. You have to let go of everything that ever was even a little bit to do with it.

Sue: My daughter said once, "If you really knew me, you wouldn't love me." What do you think she meant?

Olivia: ...oh, this is going to make me cry...people with an eating disorder don't love themselves and they feel that what's inside of them isn't worth being loved. So, part of the reason I didn't tell my parents is because I wasn't worth the help, right?

I hate when people say, "Why don't you just stop?" And you know, I wish I could, because making myself throw up and everything that comes with it, is absolutely disgusting. It makes you feel so ashamed, so worthless, so disgusting physically and mentally. It tires you out more than anything. I can't even begin to explain the shame I feel for what I've done to myself. So I think that's it: What I am doing isn't loveable. Who I am, because I'm doing that, isn't worth being loved. The thoughts I have aren't loveable.

[The illness] is selfish and mean. It's mainly really selfish. You revolve around you. I don't think: "I should get better for my parents." No, I think: "I don't feel good, I'm going to throw up." [The eating disorder] is constantly saying: "What do you want? What do you want?!" Not: "Think about how this is affecting everyone around you." Obviously, you think about that, but it's not enough to stop you.

I think the main thing to realize, especially after a couple of years of being in it, is it's no longer just not feeling good enough. It's so much worse than that. It's so much worse, because people's eating disorders are so obsessive and they are so addicted. I don't just "not feel good enough", I obsess over that until I literally feel like a piece of dirt. It gets so deep. It's not just like, "Oh, what you said really hurt me." It's like: "I am that. What you just told me is right." You don't have that shield where you can say, "What you're saying isn't right. I know myself better." Everything that is said to you is absorbed.

- **What have you learned about your family?**

They're really strong, especially my mom. I know it affects her, she doesn't show me that, which helps. For my meetings and stuff, she's always the one who's sitting next to me, totally calm and I'm always the one worried about getting weighed. She's totally like, "It's fine." When I dropped a couple of pounds last year, my doctor was like, "This isn't good." My mom was like,

"It's okay, give us a few of weeks, we're going to work through it." So that was a lot better than her being like, "WHAT? What happened??!" Her just being the calm support for me really helps a lot.

• Have there been any gifts from this experience?

One gift is definitely compassion for people. I definitely feel for people who are dealing with things that some people don't see as medical issues. I feel for those people who sometimes just have to sit at home alone, because I know what that feels like. I am not going to be one of those people anymore saying, "Oh, they are just making up excuses." Because I realize there are serious issues... that not everybody knows about.

I'm stronger probably now. I realize, back when it first started, I thought that [bulimia] was the only way to fix everything. But now, through therapy and stuff, I realize that things are okay when I didn't think they were before.

When I was really young, I was also on a lot of medication for anxiety disorder and I've been on antidepressants for a long time. Just knowing that that's okay, that's part of my road to being okay. It's fine now [to take medication], whereas before I hated it. It made me feel "not normal" and when you're 12, it's important [to feel normal].

There are some days where I feel like a five-year-old. I could cry like this (*snaps fingers*). There are some days my back hurts constantly, and I know it's because of throwing up. Things like that are really hard on me. The biggest thing is feeling really fragile, if someone touched me, I could break. That's how I feel some days.

Sue: Well, I think you're amazing. You're doing incredibly hard work and your parents are so proud of you.

Olivia: Thanks. It is hard. I wish I could say it wasn't. Probably right now is the hardest part, because I see my future and, obviously, I want to be able to get there. I still have downs and ups, downs and ups. I want it to be all better, right now, but that's not going to happen. The hardest part right now is [to] keep telling myself it does still get better.

Sue: Did you see glimmers of hope along the way to recovery?

Olivia: There's really little things, like eating my lunch and not feeling bad after. Or eating dinner and not feeling so full that I just want to die. Or looking in the mirror and saying, "Wow, you look really good today." It's those little things that are like, 'OK, I can do it.'

Sue: Thanks for being so brave and sharing all this with me.

RESEARCH SAYS

Eating disorders are on the rise in children. Preteen hospitalization of children with eating disorders increased 119% between 1996 and 2006. Children as young as eight or nine are developing eating disorders.

www.elementsbehaviouralhealth.com/eating-disorders

"People with bulimia often show an increased concern over mistakes and doubts regarding actions. They often have unrealistic, self-imposed standards, self scrutiny, requiring perfection, even as compared to people with depressive or anxiety disorders."
(Castro Fornieles et al, 2007)

According to a study by Gilboa & Schechtman in 2006, people with bulimia often "mislabel aversive physical and emotional states as 'feeling fat' and focus on negative aspects of their body in order to avoid emotional experiences." They often "have difficulty identifying feelings and triggers associated with binge-purge episodes."

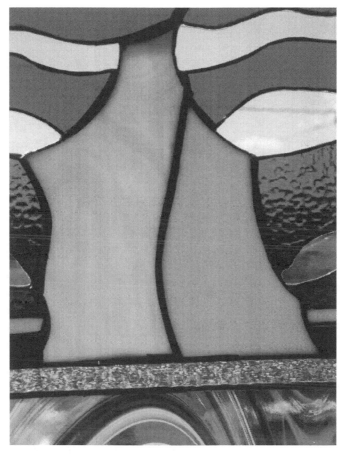

STAINED GLASS ORIGINAL: PENNY WOODING

Ryan and Kim (Olivia's parents)

"I kept telling myself it's the disease, it's not her." — Kim

"I need help. Those three words were enough hope
for me: I need help." — Ryan

Sue: How would you describe your journey, getting to today?

Kim: Scary, totally out of my element, fearful. A real lack of support,
I think, in the medical community until you get to the right people, which
takes a long time. I just think having a teenager is so tough to begin with
and then you don't know what parts are part of the disease and what part
is being a teenager. And so that was sort of the struggle. Every little thing,
you're wondering, "Is this part of this illness or is it just because she's a
teenager?" The biggest thing has been my fear for her. Wanting so badly
for your child to be happy and successful and socially accepted and all of
those things and worrying that some of those things won't happen for her.

When they are little and things are bothering them or they get hurt you
can just pick them up and hug them or put a *Barbie Band-Aid* on it and
everything is fine. But when they get to this stage, you can't always just
fix it with a hug and that's hard. The way I used to fix things isn't working
anymore... it's a whole new learning curve.

Ryan: My answer is going to be completely different. The journey, for me, has been relief. I come from a background with a lot of mental illness. Most of the people in my life that have a mental illness think it's everywhere else instead of inside of them. So when Olivia came to us looking for help, that was a real eye-opener, it was awesome, because I've never seen that before.

And I guess the other thing is I've learned, the hard way, that you can't fix this stuff. There is no fixing it. What I mean by that is if you're standing on the outside as a parent or a brother or as a son and you might think, 'I can do something about this'... and then the realization comes that you can't do anything. Basically, you're an observer to what's going on. You can support people but you can't change them; you can't fix anything. All the stuff has to come from within themselves. One hundred percent.

• Overview

Kim: It was probably January 2011 [2.5 years ago], we started just noticing that she was not herself. We found her in her room, lighters in her back pack, she was always sort of explaining things away, and getting depressed and finally I just said to her one day... I yelled at her, "What the hell is going on? Who are you? I don't know who you are! You need to tell me what is going on!" She just lost it and said, "I've been making myself throw up. I'm really not happy." And we sat and cried for a longtime and then I said, "What do we need to do?" And she said, "I need help" and I said, "Yes." The next day I had her at the pediatrician and then he put in the request for her to go see Dr. O, but it was ten months for her to get in.

She was 15. We were lucky in that we caught it: she'd lost a little bit of weight but not significant, so it wasn't like she was at risk physically, yet. She said it had been going on for a couple of months and she'd also done it one other time, for a few of months that I didn't know anything about.

So we went to the pediatrician every week for her to be weighed and he tried to talk to her, but he had no idea really what he was doing. I mean he wasn't trained and he would just say look on the chart and say, "You are fine, but you know that isn't good [to throw up]." And I was like, "Oh Lord! You're not helping." When we found out it was going to be such a long wait [to get into see Dr. O], I said to her, "I'm going to find you someone in the meantime." We were able to find a psychologist in the west end, a female, that she went to for a while until we were able to get into the University [Hospital] and that helped. Just someone to get her talking.

October 2011, she got in [to the U of A Eating Disorder Unit]. So it's been just over a year since treatment started. I mean we were lucky in many ways she never had to be admitted. Dr. O talked to her a few times about either this starts to improve now or we admit you, but we never had to. For quite a while, we were going weekly, but now she has monthly visits.

My only concern is... it's all about the food and the bingeing but there still isn't enough about the underlying psychological issues and that concerns me. So I need to talk to Dr. O about that. She's on the *Prozac* and she may not be throwing up as much—I still think she does it—but that's just the side effect of the disease and I'm not sure she's really being treated enough for the core issues. I'm afraid it will just come out in something else: if I'm not going to throw up, then I'll start cutting or I'll start doing something else. Until you get the psychological part... just taking *Prozac*, it's helpful, yes, but it's not enough.

Ryan: I remember the beginning of it. I remember I was really scared. From my personal experience, I just saw another chapter of the genetic train. To be honest with you, I think a number of people in my family have undiagnosed mental illnesses, including myself. You always hear about how sometimes it jumps a generation and, in my brain, I was kind of hoping, "Please nobody have to go through the crap I've seen with my mom, my dad, my sister — please no — " and then when it happened, that was a devastation in itself.

Kim: For the first six months or so, we didn't know where we were going or how this was going to end up. Both her and I. Her not being able to control herself and me watching her struggling with it. She felt like she needed to throw up, she knew she shouldn't. If she didn't, she was full of anxiety; if she did, she felt better temporarily, but it's not a fix that you want them to be using. And not knowing, not able to just do something. The hardest thing is feeling powerlessness. What can I DO? I can force her to go to her appointments and drive her there. That's the only thing I can really do. That was hard, that was really hard. Not being able to get in her brain and help to figure it out.

Ryan: Another thing that was a bit of an obstacle for her—she's a competitive dancer. That was tough. There was point when Dr. O said, "I don't know where we should go with this. Dancing is not a good environment for a person with an eating disorder to be in." All the people around you are in similar mode or are reinforcing the fact that the skinnier you are, the better you are. And we said, "Well, it's the only thing she is enjoying right now; she loves being there." And Kim was really, really adamant right from the beginning: "We are not punishing you. This is not punishment. You came to us and told us what your problem is, we're going to get you help. At no time are you going to hear us say, " 'Why are you doing this? You're screwing up.' "

So we had a dilemma, because the doctor's saying that the dancing is probably not a great environment, but if we took it away that would look like punishment. One of the things that happened, the dietician explained to her the physiology: this is what you're eating and this is what you're burning. You're killing yourself internally. You're burning 3X calories and you're eating X. And you're doing it every day. Do the math.

Kim: So that was a hard decision. There were many hard moments.

Ryan: Kim did an amazing job, and I know it was really tough for her. There was that moment after we would eat and Olivia would get up and go upstairs and Kim would be right behind her. The whole time you don't know how this is going to turn out. Is she going to turn around and scream at us to "Get out my life, you're ruining my life!" You're walking into something and you want to see what's there, but you don't want to see it. You're hoping like hell. "I don't want you to think I'm following up here because I don't trust you, but I want you to know that I don't want you coming up here to do something destructive and I see what you're doing." Again, is it discipline or is it help?

Sue: Trust is a huge issue, because there is so much lying and secrecy involved to protect the illness. How did you overcome that feeling of betrayal?

Kim: I kept trying to tell myself, 'It's the disease, it's not her.' Even though it would break my heart, the things she would say: "I hate you. You are the worst mom. Leave me alone, it's my life." The knife is going in and out of your heart. I cried a lot. But I kept trying to tell myself, 'It's not her, that's not her voice that's talking right now.'

But I still don't think I'm completely over it. Even the last little while, she's eating supper and going upstairs. And, oh, so I'm back up there. It's been so long. I want to trust, but I don't. I still look through her backpack and her purses. Check to see where she's going and who she is with.

Ryan: And if she's eating. "Let me see your lunch."

Kim: Sometimes I'll change her sandwich. She's very structured, with food especially. She eats the same thing everyday, everyday. So I'll forget to put the lettuce in and then I'll ask, "Did you notice what I did wrong with your sandwich today?" and sometimes she's like, "No...." [meaning: she didn't eat it]

Or she goes to the mall with her friends, "Where did you guys go? Did you have anything to eat?" kind of in a conversational way. I don't trust her completely. I don't think I can. Not that I don't want to trust her, but I'm afraid to. I don't want to think that she's recovered and I can slip back because I know how easily it can go the other way again. So I think you always have to have that awareness.

• How would you define recovery?

Kim: I think I'm hoping she can learn how to deal in healthier ways with anxiety and stress. To learn that there are options besides harming yourself physically. She will always have mental health issues. She's not just going to recover and be someone different. It's something she's dealt with forever, since she was born. She was a child, right from the beginning, that was full of anxiety and stress. So that's not going to change. I think I need for her to be able to manage it herself and accept that it's something that she is going to have for the rest of her life and that that's OK. It's no different than having diabetes or having another type of illness, you just need to learn to manage and you need to look for what things are your stressors.

She's learning that everyone has something. Everybody's got some issues. That's part of the maturing. You know, when you are 13, 14, 15, your brain works in a way that you think that everyone is always looking at you and you're the centre of everybody's universe and people are defining you. As you mature, you start to understand that there's a whole world around you and that you're not The Only One, that everyone has issues. And she's starting to get that, she'll say, "I know everyone's got something they are dealing with."

- ### Is *recovery* the wrong word?

Kim: When I think of someone who's recovered, I think of someone who doesn't have that disease anymore. If someone is recovered from cancer or an injury, it's gone, but this is not something that's gone. Hopefully the eating disorder part of it, she can recover from that, but the underlying issues that caused her to go to that as her outlet, she's not going to recover from that—that's part of who she is. She just needs to learn that that's only a small part of her and that it doesn't define who she is and who she becomes.

Ryan: Is it okay if I just agree with her? Because that's exactly what I was going to say. I think it's the difference between when they say 'You quit smoking' or 'You stop smoking'. I think you just stop, I don't think you ever quit. I don't think you quit being mentally ill, that's part of you. There's no way. It's like she said—it's part of you. There's chemical issues and there's environmental issues that maybe you can sway a bit, but at the end of the day, it's more how you cope.

Kim: It's as much a genetic thing as anything else. Being born with blonde hair, you can colour your hair and be a brunette, but you're still always a blonde. You are always going to have that.

- ## What gave you hope?

Kim: Her willingness to talk about what she's going through gave me hope, because I thought if she can tell me she's sad or she's had a bad day, that those were hopeful things. It's when they're holding them inside and taking them out in a destructive way that you worry. So even if she would say, "I just need to go into my room for a while because I had a bad day." "OK, great. When you're ready, I'm here. I'll talk to you." I would rather that. And that would give me hope.

And then she'd come down and say, "I let something stupid bother me and I shouldn't have." Just those little things. Or when she wants to talk, the next day: "What happened yesterday was this or that." And I'll feel bad for her, I'll have empathy for her for what happened, but inside I'm like, "Yeah!! She's talking to me." Those are hopeful things. Because for a long time, she wasn't telling us what was going on, and that was the scary thing: that I didn't know. So when she verbalises the bad as well as the good, that gives me hope.

Ryan: We would always go do the appointments with Dr. O, Olivia first and then Kim and I would go in after. We wouldn't spend a lot of time together in the room. I remember once: "Hi Dr. O. How are you?" "Not too bad, just want to let you know that Olivia said she got sick six times this week." Kim and I would look at each other. I'd go, "Did you know that?" She'd go, "No."

But! But!! Forget the disappointment of 'Oh my God, how come I didn't know that?' I DO know that, why do I know that? Because she told her doctor!! She's comfortable in this environment. She TOLD HER! I know it's really crappy news, but that's awesome that she *said something*!

Sue: Thank you for sharing that with me. I really needed a different perspective. Whenever I get bad news, I immediately go to a dark place: "I screwed up. I wasn't supervising properly." I never think: "She told her doctor. Isn't that great?" That's a whole new thought for me.

Kim: *She told somebody.* If she's not telling you, but if she's telling the doctor, she's still asking for help. She may not be asking you, but if she's willing to tell the doctor, she's telling someone that she knows is going to help her. And that's saying she feels value in herself, that she wants that help and support from someone. And as much as we always want it to be us, sometimes I think the weight of all that maybe gets to be too much. Sometimes, I'm like, I don't know if I could have taken that news today, so let Dr. O take that weight on her shoulders and give me a couple of days to breathe again and then I'll get back into it.

Ryan: Just the fact that she sought out help. I think it tells me that later in her life, when she needs help, she'll say, "Hey the last time...." Because it was scary what she did, that was really scary, for her to come forward at that time. I commend her a ton for that. So that's the most hopeful thing for me, and again because it's so foreign to my experience. I've heard it time and time again from my family: "Everybody hates me, everybody's against me, it's just me against the world." But not: "I need help."

Those three words were enough hope for me: I need help.

• What were the turning points in her journey?

Ryan: When she originally went to go and see the dietician, she gave Olivia the cards and she said, "You gotta eat this, you gotta eat that." And Olivia was very skeptical. She thought if she ate anything that wasn't lettuce, she was going to balloon. So when she went in and did the cards, and dedicated herself as good as she could to the regiment the first week and then was weighed, and—if I'm not mistaken—she actually lost weight. I think she thought: 'Wow, like Wow! I'm not a blimp. I ate. I actually ate meat, I have breakfast, and I had snack and did all this stuff that I told myself I couldn't do. I need this food.' I think that was probably huge for her. It dispelled a rumour that if she was to have that hamburger, she'd be done.

Kim: I think, too, with regards to the medication, at first, she didn't want to take it. She thought it was going to make her tired. She didn't want to be taking pills. We were away one day and I said to her, "Did you take your pills?" and she said, "Yes" and then later on in the afternoon, she started to not feel well and she said to me, "I didn't tell you the truth. I forgot to take my medicine and now I don't feel very good." She thought: "I really do need to take them." When they upped her dose, she started to get tremors and so we had to cut her dose. And then she said to me a couple of weeks later, "You know, I felt better when I was taking more. Other than the tremors, I felt better. I think I need to find a way to get back to that dosage." The fact that she recognized that she needed it and that it was working for her, took away her fear of doing it. She saw it as a tool to feeling better.

Ryan: There's a stigma too, I imagine. I'm not going to put words in her [Olivia's] mouth. For me, if someone said to me, "You got to take *Prozac*", I would probably consider it a negative thing next to my name. So I would agree that there's a point where she put aside her concerns that were superficial. They went away when she saw it actually helped her.

Kim: Certainly she had times where it was really dark, where [she felt] nothing was going to help and she was always going to be like this. So you had to battle through those days and hold your breath and hope and hope and hope that she can find her way out of those days.

• How would you define hope?

Ryan: Is it like faith? I dunno. Maybe for me, it's kind of like faith. What I mean by that is it's something you don't control. I have faith in a lot of things, but I don't have control over any of them. My faith is based on: I think the world will be like this tomorrow. I think my wife will still be in my house. I think my key will still work in the door when I come back from a two-week job on the road. I think Olivia has the ability to deal with her issues. That might sound simplistic, but for me that's the best way to say it. Blind faith.

Kim: People say, "I hope it doesn't rain." It doesn't always hold the proper amount of weight. When I think of hope, I think of just a brightness, a sunshine, a... I don't know. It's hard. It's a bigger thing to me. To have hope is to want to grab onto a rainbow and be happy. It's a hard word to describe.

If you say, "Well I hope she has a great future," that doesn't carry with it that she has the ability to control that or I have the ability to help her have that better future. It's not just "Well, I hope" and "Hopefully it will happen". There has to be the work behind it, too.

And I think you have to look for the little successes because it's not a journey that you're going to wake up tomorrow and go, "Oh! Everything is great!" I think you really have to [look]—and sometimes you have to search really hard—to find something little. Try and reinforce the little, itty, bitty, tiny steps that are taken. Something like: Wow! It only took her seven minutes to get dressed for school today. Or: She went to bed, knowing what she was going to wear, and she got up in the morning and she put it on and she didn't say it makes me look fat and I would be like, "*Woohoo!*" And I would try to acknowledge those things with her, without going overboard, because you can get yourself so wrapped up in it. I think they sense that too and then for them it's like, 'I just disappointed them again. I'm making my mom sad.' I think you have to acknowledge that those feelings are there, but I think you can't buy into it too much, because that's what they're doing.

• Life now?

Kim: Now is good. Now is good. She's planning for her future. She's excited about grad. She got her acceptance letter to the university the other day. She knows the path she's taking. She feels better about herself. We don't hear the negative talk as much. We definitely have a lot more good days than bad, or good hours than bad hours because, still, it's not always a day. It can start off great and turn really fast, but the percentage is definitely higher of good.

As a parent, there's still that fear in the back of my mind, but I'm proud of her, with everything she's gone through. I'm really proud of her for how hard she's worked, that she's stuck with it and fought through it. I'm really proud of the woman that she has become. And hoping I had some small part in that. Other than just the genetics!

Ryan: For the last ten years, I've been physically absent, a lot. My job takes me away from home 180 days a year. There's definitely an interesting dynamic, being away for two weeks, and then walking in the house and saying, "Oh, why are you doing this? You should be doing this."

Let's just say that when the door opened, and Kim and Olivia both invited me in, basically saying, "We want you at all the doctor's appointments, even if you are just sitting there," that was really cool, because it showed that I wasn't just participating from afar. It's a lot better for me because I feel a lot more engaged. Maybe I haven't felt engaged before—and maybe it's 'cuz I'm a guy—I honestly believe that there is some kind silly thing in my brain that says I can fix everything. Sometimes, I just can't say, "Sorry, that sucks." Instead it's: "Hang on, I'll be right over! Let me get on the ladder!"

So for me, life now is a lot better. I've seen a positive outcome. I'm seeing Olivia really grow in the last year. Sometimes you hear about kids who kind of fall off the path and they are hurting themselves in many different ways and they don't know how to stop. I think Olivia is going to be a really great adult. She's going to look after herself. She's going to know that it's OK to say, "Hey, I need help." That's a gift for me.

The other thing too is sharing time, because, I mean, at that stage of her life, maybe there's not so much time spent with a teenaged girl and her dad, talking about stuff. So that was a gift too, because there was actual structured time going to the doctor or whatever. I guess it's easy to see the gifts today because we feel like we've jumped the hurdle and got to the other side.

Kim: I think in many ways, it was a good experience for Olivia and me because we talked a lot more about how she was really feeling inside than I would have otherwise. And we did spend a lot more time together and I'm hopeful that, going forward, she knows that she has us and some other members of the family that love her no matter what stage she's going through. I think she knows that and she sees that support. She's become a very strong person. She's become very hopeful for the future. She's got her plans. There was times when I thought, 'Please just talk about something in the future' because I was so concerned. There were times when she would say, "You would be happier if I wasn't here. Maybe I should just die." You just want them to talk about something in the future, that they are thinking ahead... and she is now.

Ryan: For her to say, "Wow, I'm really looking forward to this dance competition, I'm really looking forward to this wedding, I want to go to nursing school..." She's thinking forward, which is really cool. She has things she wants to accomplish.

Kim: It's always a work in progress and what worked last week may not work next week, but you have to know there's something that will work, always. You just have to wade through the other stuff to find it.

Ryan: The gift was "Oh my God, somebody navigated through this water!" And as Kim said, they're not recovered, but they actually found some way to swim upstream, whereas everybody else—and no offence to them—but everyone else I know who's been in this pool has not swam, they've just let the current take them. I think Olivia, of all the people I know with a mental illness, she's the strongest, by far. By far.

The aims of treatment for patients with bulimia nervosa are to:

1 reduce and, where possible, eliminate binge eating and purging;

2 treat physical complications of bulimia nervosa;

3 engage patient's motivation to cooperate in restoration of healthy eating patterns and participate in treatment;

4 provide education regarding healthy nutrition and eating patterns;

5 help patients reassess and change core dysfunctional thoughts, attitudes, motives, conflicts and feelings related to the eating disorder;

6 treat associated psychiatric conditions, including deficits in mood and impulse regulation, self-esteem and behaviour;

7 enlist family support and provide family counseling and therapy where appropriate; and

8 prevent relapse.

Early recognition of eating disorder symptoms and early intervention may prevent an eating disorder from becoming chronic.

— *The Practice Guideline for the Treatment of Patients with Eating Disorders*, Third Edition, 2006 American Psychiatric Association
www.pysch.org

Roommates

Despite increasing her caloric intake, week after week, Hannah wasn't gaining weight. She was supervised for almost every waking minute of her day, either at the 4F4 day program or at home. Every time she went to the bathroom, someone was standing outside the door, listening for any sounds of purging. (There weren't any) We couldn't figure out why she wasn't gaining weight.

Based on a tip I read in the book *Help Your Teenager Beat an Eating Disorder* (Lock & leGrange), I started sleeping her room. Hannah didn't want me there, on a mattress on the floor, inches away from her bed—what teenager would—but she didn't fight me as much as I expected. And slowly she began to gain weight, so we were room-mates for about two months. Finally, the time came for me to "move out". I remember the first few nights back in my own room, I lay awake most of the night, listening for sounds. Many months later, Hannah confessed that, before I started sleeping in her room, she had been getting up at 4:00 AM and exercising for hours, before I came in to "wake her up" at 6:30 AM. She said she wouldn't have been able to stop, without me being there.

There are times when we, as parents, have to step in and create the human barrier between our child and their illness, because they are too weak to fight it alone. And then, there is that difficult moment when you have to give them the reins again... let them try, let them fail, help them back up and let them try again.

PHOTO: EILEEN SPROULE

Hailey and Val

A daughter (Hailey) and her mother (Val) talk about their seven-year journey together, battling Hailey's eating disorder. This was the only interview I did with both participants at the same time. Hailey was 22 at the time of the interview.

"There were overdoses, there was cutting, drinking, not eating. Oh, the chaos. The absolute chaos." —Val

"It's such a weird feeling to be absolutely terrified of yourself." —Hailey

Val: Do you want to go first?

Hailey: I can try. It started with simple depression and anxiety. I had a friend that self-harmed and I started to do that as a way of coping with the really bad feelings. When I was 15, I started restricting and exercising a lot and it just took on a world of its own. I was an outpatient when I was 16–17 for about a week in total because I never went. Then about three years ago, Dr. O suggested I be an inpatient. At first I wasn't OK with it at all. I was like, "No way. You can't make me. I'm 19. No." But my parents—I live at home for free—and they said, "It's this or you're out." So that was the only reason I went into the hospital, it's the only reason I got better because I was kind of forced to. And I know everyone is like, "You have to do it on your own" and stuff like that, but when you are at a low weight, a critically low weight, you have to go in, because you can't think. You can't think at all.

Now, I've been out of the hospital for a year and a half and I see Dr. O still at least twice a month, sometimes more. And it's still hard, but I always can go back there if I need to, for support.

Val: And you email.

Hailey: Oh yeah, I email her all the time.

Val: As a parent, there's lots you don't know. I mean I thought I did, but I didn't. Between Grade 9 and Grade 10 is a crucial time. I remember going to the Open House for high school and she walked in the front door, right down the hall and out the other end. She did not want to go, at all. She had really high anxiety coupled with depression. Then in Grade 10, she had a boyfriend, there were arguments, typical teenage angst. She couldn't deal with the teenaged angst like most kids do, which would be—I don't know—writing in a diary or getting drunk or whatever they do. Hailey was kind of always socially younger. In Grade 10, she quit going to school. She'd pretend she was going to school, and she'd jump on a bus and go down to Whitemud [Equine Centre], where her horse was. Then a boy said something in Grade 10... remember some boy saying you had fat hips or something?

Hailey: Oh yeah, I was complaining about how I felt fat, and all that, just like a normal girl, and one of my friends was like, "You're not fat at all. You just have really, really curvy hips for someone your age." And that was it. It was a compliment, but I didn't take it that way, at all.

Val: Yeah, because your self-esteem was low. So in Grade 10, I took her to a pediatric psychiatrist at the Royal Alex [Hospital] and he said, "She has ADHD." And that's where the problem started... .

Hailey (*interjecting*): Oh yeah!! *Adderall!!*

Val: ...because what did he give her for ADHD? *Adderall.*

Sue: What is that?

Val: It's a stimulant.

Hailey and Val (*at the same time*): It's cocaine in a pill.

Hailey: It kills your appetite for three days after one dosage.

Val: A lot of the girls are on it.

Hailey: It hypes you up.

Val: This psychiatrist says, "Oh, the reason she can't concentrate at school is because she has ADHD." So when he gave her that, she started losing weight and then what did people say? "Oh! You look really good. You've lost a few pounds." She never was heavy. She's always been petite. But the *Adderall* was, for me, the biggest problem. And I should know better, as a nurse, but it worked: her marks were fantastic. I was home schooling by this point and she would get through a whole booklet in an afternoon. That's when it started and got progressively worse. When she came down [off the medication] there was self-harm issues. It really started getting bad.

Homeschooling was like pulling teeth and I said, "You don't have to go to high school, but you need to get your high school," which was a mistake for me, because I gave into the anxiety. I should have moved schools, like you did. But she told me this morning that she wouldn't have gone anyway, which made me feel better. It did.

Hailey: Hindsight.

Sue: It's soul-destroying.

Hailey: It is.

Val: It's a dangerous place to go.

Val: (*about hindsight*) You do reach a point where all of the sudden, you go, *Bing!* 'Just a minute here. I'm bullying myself. I did the very best I could, that I knew how.' The psychiatrist she's seeing now says there are so many circumstances outside of the home that make these girls take this route, it's not just mom and dad, or a boyfriend. It's so many things, like social media...social media is really bad, eh?

Hailey: Yeah, Facebook and stuff.

Val: Then they hit the pro-ana sites and it takes on a whole world of its own.

It was bad; I didn't even know who she was. I got her into Dr. O and she got her off the *Adderall*, which was very difficult.

Hailey: Dr. O had to call two other doctors and insist they stop prescribing me this medication.

Val: Somewhere on Netcare, in her chart, it said she had ADHD, so...

Hailey: I'd just go to the Medicentre and show them my old bottle of *Adderall* and say I need some more.

Val: They'd just throw anything at her. They just want her out of the office. Kids sell *Adderall* too. Anywhere you buy pot, you can also get *Adderall*, and *Ativan*, and *Xanax* and cocaine.

Hailey: Absolutely anything in the world you want.

Val: And when they take the *Adderall* away, they sometimes try the cocaine. A lot of that goes on, on the Unit, with the older women.

Hailey: I got it taken it away but then I met a girl on the Unit, Susan, who is now my best friend, and her mom happens to be a doctor and happens to keep her prescription pad at home and happens not to notice when I take as many I want. So that's when I started making prescriptions: *Adderall*, *Adderall*, *Ativan*, whatever. Then we got caught by Dr. O from someone on the Unit and she called Susan's mom and that was the end of that.

Val: And me. She told me about it.

Hailey: And then she called the pharmacy and put a block on my *Adderall* refill. So that was done.

Val: Now pharmacies are all on one computer, so it doesn't matter... anywhere you go in Canada, that block will show up, so there are good things. But we are getting ahead of ourselves. (*takes a breath*)

• University

Val: First year University, she was very, very ill because of the restricting. (*to Hailey*) You were so irritable, so mean... she wasn't even the same person. We threw thousands and thousands of dollars at courses, to let her to try again and again. She never went to school, she'd always skip, she'd never show up. She'd go to the gym instead or go riding. Her entire first year was a wash. 6–7 thousand dollars just out the window. Then we got fed up. We got to a point where we said, "OK, enough! No more outpatient therapy." Because they don't go to the outpatient, anyway. You think they are going, but they're not going. You drop them off at the front door and they go out.

Hailey: Yeah, even on Close Observation. You just walk off. The Unit Security guard didn't pay attention.

Val: I think when it came to, like Hailey said, the ultimatum, was when we said: "OK, this is it. No more chances. You go into the hospital or we're done." There was overdoses. There was cutting. Restricting and getting drunk and then the problems that go with that. I mean, she'd go to a nightclub, drink on an empty stomach and her boyfriend would get violent because she talks to someone else. Oh, the chaos. Absolute chaos!

Hailey: Oh yeah. You wouldn't even believe it. This is the nice version of it.

Val: You're right, it is.

Hailey: It is.

Val: There was drunk driving and smoking weed in the car. I'd get up at 4 o'clock in the morning to use the bathroom and the truck would be gone. I didn't know where she was. She had no cognitive ability, because she was starving to death, and I knew that. She'd be gone out all hours of night. She'd be missing. We'd take away the keys to the car, she'd go on foot. She was just out of control. And she knows it. You were...

Hailey: Yeah, I just think... I dunno... you are talking about this story like you lived it, and a lot of the details are very, very off. They are your opinion.

Val: Yeah, my perspective.

Hailey: It's very different from what actually happened. So I'm trying to keep my mouth shut.

Val: No, don't, don't. Say it. "She was overbearing" or whatever, tell her. It's okay.

Sue: That's why we I want to interview both of you—to get both perspectives. It's really important to hear both. The truth is probably...

Val & Hailey (*at the same time*) ...somewhere in between.

Hailey: I'll cut you off the next time. I keep forgetting about things that happened and then you bring something up and I think, 'Oh, right, there's something else.'

Val: OK. So we finally said, "You go to inpatient. Not only do you have to go to inpatient but you have to go to therapy, for at least a year, or we're washing our hands of this. While you're doing that, yes, we will continue to pay for as many courses as you can handle, we will continue to put gas in your car."

• Being admitted

The morning she went inpatient, I woke my husband up and I said to him, "This, I cannot do. You're on. You're taking her [to be admitted to the hospital]."

Hailey: He could hardly do it, either.

Val: "I am not going to take a suitcase and get on that elevator and go up there and leave my child there."

Hailey: In that room, yeah.

Val: "I'm not doing it. This is my line in the sand. You get up and you go do this." I mean, he did. Because, man, hey, you feel like a failure dropping your kid off there. When they were little, I had a little nutrition guide on the fridge: "Two teaspoons of vegetables, three teaspoons of meat" and then... all of sudden, this.... It's horrible leaving them there. It's hell. And then the crying. She phoned the first night, crying, crying, crying.

Hailey: "Come get me from this place. Why did you leave me here?"

Val: "Come get me. Please, Mom, I'm sick. I'm throwing up, they've locked the bathroom door and I can't..."

Hailey: I got the flu but the nurse didn't know that I was anorexic, she thought I was bulimic so she locked the bathroom, wouldn't let me go in toilet and wouldn't give me a bucket to puke in.

Val: She was just crying, crying, crying. In the middle of the night on the phone, I'm saying, "You can do this." When they're inpatients, they put them on drugs because they have anxiety about eating. The first time I went to pick her up, she was so strung out on *Seroquel*, which is an anti-psychotic. They've put my kid on an anti-psychotic! I feel like I've dropped my kid off at *The Shining* and Jack Nicholson has been looking after her. And I phoned... poor Dr. O...

Hailey: Oh yeah! You screamed at her.

Val: I was furious. I said, "This is ridiculous!! She's stoned out of her mind! I don't want to see her like this!!" And Dr. O was so good.

Hailey: She was so calm with you.

Val: She said, "This is only temporary."

Hailey: And she was right.

Val: "She's not going to stay on this [drug]." To see your kid stoned out of her mind, just so they can eat. Makes you feel so pathetic.

• What is recovery?

Hailey: It used to mean getting to a goal weight and then I hit that goal weight and I've mostly maintained it for the last two years, but I'm not, by any means, recovered. Maybe half-way recovered. Now recovery means a normal, healthy relationship with food: eating three meals a day, not feeling like killing yourself after each meal. Happiness and health and normal eating, like everyone else does. Having other things in your life. It's hard. A lot of the therapy is discovering the problems underneath that are making you do all this stuff and those things are really hard to deal with.

Val: For so long, the eating disorder owned her, and now I can honestly say she owns it. I mean, it still owns her some days. (*to Hailey*) Right?

Hailey: Yeah, some days.

Val: Some days. But on the most part, she owns it. She has control over it, rather than it having control over her. Sometimes she still slides. And exactly like she's saying, the days she slides, there's always some trigger behind it, a hurt, or an anger behind it, or slipping back into the past and punishing herself for things she may have done or ways she may have acted or been. That's why you have to get to that point where we both say: The past is past. If you go back there and you start living it over and over again, you'll go nuts and that's not progress.

Sue: So part of recovery is letting go of the past?

Hailey: Oh, yeah.

Val: Do not look in the rearview mirror. Do not look in the rearview mirror. Put your hands on the wheel and look straight ahead.

Hailey: Yeah.

Val: Because if you look in the rearview mirror, you're going to crash; because your eyes aren't going to be ahead, they're going to be in the wrong place. I often use that analogy with Hailey.

Sue: Is recovery even the right word?

Hailey: Um, I think, I don't know... recovery is an okay word for it, I guess. But the concept behind it where everyone thinks you just go into the hospital, and get better and then you eat and then you're all good. It's not like that. It's a really, really, really long journey, especially for someone who has it engraved into their habits. I feel like it's who I am, so it's really hard to get rid of, 'cuz you don't really remember a way of life before it. Recovery is an okay word but it's definitely a journey—a long one.

Val: My word is Stability. I don't think of success as recovery, I think of success as stability. That you can go out to a family function and eat a meal or a boyfriend can ask her out for dinner and she can go out—maybe eat less than someone else would, or not finish it—but still, stability. Life stability. When you are in the throes of an eating disorder, there is no stability, it is out of control. So, for me, it's the idea of re-stabilizing your life.

Hailey: [The eating disorder] helps with you cope with anxiety. I don't know why, it totalling dampens it. I have severe social anxiety—generalized anxiety disorder—and for some reason, when I'm restricting, it totally goes away. It's weird and it's screwed up, but it helps.

Val: But that's maladaptive.

Hailey: Yeah.

Val: Like anything else. It's like the guy who has to drink to socialize and becomes an alcoholic. You restrict to get rid of your social anxiety and become an anorexic. It's maladaptive behaviour. That's what she's trying to learn now. She's in DBT with an eating disorder group at the Royal Alex [Hospital], which has done more than anything.

Sue: What does DBT stand for?

Val: Dialectical Behaviour Therapy. That's something you should look into. Truly, you should. The success is unbelievable.

Hailey: It's learning skills to deal with emotional...

Val: (*finishing the sentence*) ...dysregulation.

Hailey: Pretty much.

Val: One of the diagnoses that got thrown out when Hailey was going through this, was borderline personality disorder, which you will hear along the way. A lot of the behaviours of anorexia, including self-harm, are similar to borderline personality disorder. You have emotional dysregulation problems, you have suicide attempts, you have all of those things. They've since questioned her diagnosis, but the gift for us was getting that diagnosis in the first place, because that's what got her in with Dr. Hibbard in the DBT program.

For other traumatic reasons, Hailey had a huge issue with men. But she's developed a really, really strong rapport with Dr. Hibbard, which has shown her—another gift—that there are men out there that are kind and care about her and validate her. That's another gift. (*to Hailey*) See? Gifts, gifts.

Hailey: Yeah, that's true.

Val: (*to Hailey*) It's made you and I close. We had our love-hate relationship times. My husband worked out of town, so I was always close to the kids. Too close. Sometimes.

Hailey: Yeah, it's not as bad anymore, but it definitely was too close.

Val: I was a helicopter parent.

• What you learn

I didn't need to pay [for support]—well, I went once and paid $170 to a psychologist, because I was so depressed and distraught. She told me: "Kick her out of the house, don't send her to school, no more school, don't give her any more chances, don't help her with her homework. She's got to hurt before she will figure it out." My husband said, "No way, no way." We just couldn't do it. It's like kicking out somebody who has MS or something. It's really a disease.

Hailey: Yeah, I mean, I wasn't safe to be by myself.

Val: Yeah, she would have killed herself, because she tried that several times when she was starving her brain. In the end, you're still a mother and you still have an instinct about what is right and what is wrong and you need to listen to that, because it will steer you in the right direction.

You definitely learn things... who jams out on ya'!! Really! She learned too, with friends and boyfriends: who jams out on you when the chips are down. The people who don't really think it's a disease; they think you're doing it on purpose or you're attention-seeking or whatever. They are cruel. They were really cruel. A lot of people.

• Impact on the family

I learned that my husband is super-sensitive. He's a tough red-neck but he's a puddle with her. So okay, I have to put that aside. It is very hard on marriages. Little things like he says, "Quit bitching at her." And I say, "You've been away for two weeks, she's been out every night, writing *Adderall* prescriptions and..."

PHOTO: JENNY HAWKINS

Sue: It's hard to get on the same page. In the middle of a crisis.

Val: Especially if one spouse works out of town a lot. I was always doing it alone. And the siblings too, they are affected. Her twin brother he was mad, so mad at her for having this. To go up to the Unit to see her just about killed him.

Hailey: He came and saw me once and I was inpatient for a month and a half. So I saw him once in that month and a half.

Val: That was so hard.

Hailey: We've never been away from each other for more than a week. We're best friends. We never fight. It's crazy. So that was shitty. I didn't get to see him, kind of like, 'If you want to choose the eating disorder, then I'm not going to be there.' It was so hard.

Val: That's your perspective. His perspective was what is happening to her, is happening to me. He said, "If there's something wrong with her, then there's something wrong with me. If she's sick, then I'm sick." So the closer he got to her, the sicker he felt. It was really weird. He wasn't eating too. He was totally anorexic too. He probably wasn't eating more than 500 calories a day when she was sick. And as she's recovered, he's recovered. He's eating better than he ever has, as she recovered. It was something else. I tell you, it's bizarre.

So the dynamic—the family dynamic—is affected when you have an eating disorder... the sick child gets all the attention. Our whole house for five years was centered around her. Her brother was a good student, straight-A student and playing in a band. He should have been getting a lot of recognition, but he didn't get anything because I didn't have time or energy for it. So I feel badly about that. There's that guilt, again.

Hailey: Yeah, the guilt is very hard.

Val: Yeah for sure it is and then they get the guilt when they get better. They don't reward themselves for all the progress they've made. They just think, 'How could I have done that... why did I treat them that way?'

Hailey: Well, um, I felt that way when I had my eating disorder too, it just drove my eating disorder to get worse and worse. It was liking using an excuse to get sicker.

Val: Well, it's just another form of self-harm. It begins that way and then it just takes on a life of its own.

• The hardest parts

Hailey: Um, the entire thing was terrible. But I know the worst pain and the worst hurt and depression I've ever felt in my entire life was when it first started. And I just remember sitting in my room and I was just so, so, so worried that I was going to kill myself. I was scared of myself because I wanted to [commit suicide], so badly. And it's such a weird feeling to be absolutely terrified of yourself, where you just want to get away from yourself. It's the worst thing.

And if we are talking more recently, um, probably recovery is the worst part. It's the best part, but it's also the hardest part. All your clothes and everything doesn't fit and there's so much, so much shit that sucks. It's hard.

Val: Somebody said to me along the line—maybe it was Dr. O who said, "When she's going like this uuuuupp (*raises hand up in the air*), you're doing the same thing. So you are useless together. You are no good for her." Because of the codependency thing.

Hailey: But it's hard to step back, especially when your kid is hurting.

Val: Yeah. I used to stalk her around the house: "Why are you so sad? Why are you so sad? I want to make you happy. Come back. Come upstairs. Don't go down there. Don't lock your door. Please open your door. What are you doing in there?" I mean, it was ridiculous!!

Hailey: Sitting on my bed for eight hours, while I slept, to make sure I was okay.

Val: It was 24 hours a day. And then there was texting, and then there was, "Where are you now?" And I had all her friends programmed on my phone: "Where is she? What's she doing? Who is she talking to? Is she okay? Is she drunk? Who's bringing her home?" It was insanity! And then going to work as a nurse at 7 o'clock in the morning when you're been up 'til 5:30 looking for your child.

Oh, that time you went to the bar and I phoned your phone repeatedly: phoned it, phoned it, phoned it. No answer, no answer, no answer! And finally some guy answers and says, "I found the phone in the bar" and all I could see—and being a nurse and having seen some really horrible things—all I could see is someone picked her up off the dance floor and carried her away and she's gone. It's over. That feeling??! Unbelievable feeling. Unbelievable. And I had that over and over again. So I think what I had was—and I still have—is post traumatic stress. So when I get up in the morning and she's not here or I text her and she doesn't text back, I'm like, "Oh my God...now what?"

Hailey: Yeah, lately we've had some problems with that. Because I'm almost 22 and she'll call me at 5:30 : "Where are you?" "Well, I'm walking the dog" and she says, "No, you're not." "Yeah, I am." She knows all these bad things I was doing before. She has to understand I've changed.

Val: It takes a while to pull out of that. This is an evolution.

• How did you overcome those obstacles?

Val: Wine probably! (*laughs*) I drank a lot of wine in the six years.

Hailey: You have to think about the things in your life that mean a lot to you. For me, I have a little cousin, Mary, that I've pretty much raised her entire life. And I couldn't let myself not recover because then I would die and I wouldn't be there for her. I'm like her entire world and I know that. But... but... I don't know... then that makes me worried, hey, because what if something happened to her, then where would I be?

Val: That's all part of the process. Feeling worth it, all by yourself, in your own self, right? And that's what she has to work on now. That I'm doing this for me, not for Mary or not for the boyfriend I was trying to get back or not for Mom and Dad because they're on me. It's funny because you make them do it—and we did, we gave her an ultimatum—but somewhere along the way, they go, "Hey, this is good for me. This is what I'm supposed to be doing." And from then on, she took off.

Hailey: I don't feel like I'm there yet. I feel like I'm really terrible talking about this recovery stuff, because I'm not there yet. I don't know if I can really help with that part of it as much. I'm not fully recovered.

Sue: You may not feel like you are in the recovery zone, but when I look at you, I think you are in the recovery zone, compared to where my daughter is right now.

Val: You're very inspirational to other people.

Hailey: (*recalling a setback*) A few months ago, when I had that relapse and I was in emergency...

Val: That was probably my second lowest point. It always feels like a failure on your part, as a mother. You always feel that.

Hailey: It didn't visibly pull you down.

Val: Because the gift of this is you get stronger and stronger until you don't even know your own strength. How did I get through the setbacks? To tell you the honest truth, I don't know how I did this. I really don't. You just do. When you are going through it, you don't have time to feel sorry and have a pity party, you don't have time for that.

I was driving to the lake one time and someone phoned me, something had happened... "She was drunk and we don't know where she is. She cut herself." I can't remember who called me. There was always incidents like that. And I was driving down the highway, no word of a lie, I thought I could just veer over into an on-coming semi truck. I did reach lows like that. But I mean, you'd never do it... oh, but the things that go through your mind: 'Oh, I could just get on a plane and escape. I've got a good friend in Hawaii...'

But you don't do that because you love your kids. You are your kids. The day your kids are born, it's not about you anymore. So too bad, too bad if you were up all night and you can't sleep. Too bad. That's your job. (*pause*) Some people walk [out]. Some moms walk, some dads walk.

• Turning points

Hailey: One turning point I remember really well, when I was very sick, before I went in the hospital. My dad had this complete breakdown in the bathroom and was crying and crying and he came down to my room and he was talking to me and he's bawling his eyes out. This big man in front of me is crying! I've never seen him cry before and that was a huge, huge thing for me. He never shows any emotion. No happy, no sad. Nothing. It was really, really hard to see, and honestly, it was probably the worst moment in my entire life. I still remember it. It was so shitty. I don't want to hurt him or my family. I put them through so much, like so much.

Val: So that was a gift, though, that Dad expressed his emotions. You gave him a gift that he could do it.

Hailey: Yeah, it freaked me right out.

Sue: But you lived to tell the tale. Sometimes when you have big emotions, you think it will kill you but it's just tears.

Hailey: It's so true.

Val: Yeah it's just tears, it's just anxiety, it's just anger.....

Sue: Big feelings, for sure, but they are just feelings.

Val: And they never stay.

Sue: Are there any other turning points you remember?

Hailey: I remember the Unit actually did that for me a lot. I was in a group, every week, and there was lady there who was probably 65 years old. She was sitting there, crying, talking about her whole life: she's been hospitalized since she was 12 and talking about all this stuff. I'm thinking, 'I have to hit this hard now, because I don't want to be like that.' Seeing all these girls who are really, really sick and meeting my best friend who is really, really sick made me see this is a disease not a choice.

The very biggest turning point was when my parents told me it was own, because I really value my family relationship. Nothing was stronger than I wanted my family to love me.

Val: Another big turning point has been this program she's in now: the DBT. Because she's never done anything she didn't want to do. So when she went, and then she went again and then she went again, and she kept going. I'm like, 'Holy. Something has happened in her that has nothing to do with us.'

And that's what I want. I don't want this to do with me. I don't want this to be my problem. I don't want to go to bed with it at night, I don't want to get up with it in the morning, I don't want to see it in my kitchen. That's the worst part of this. Having something that is so toxic in your house and your life and you don't have any control over it. And it's your own home and it's your own kid and this toxic thing... you'd do anything to get rid of it, right? The biggest turning point is when she decided she's worth it. Finally. She went through a period where she was—sorry Hailey, I have to tell her this—going out with losers, because her self-esteem was so poor.

Hailey: Oh no, I know!

Val: I mean, so below her. I'm talking total losers. Where they'd walk in here and my family or girlfriends would be here and go, "Eeeek!" (*face of horror*)

Hailey: It's true.

Val: And rough guys, drug dealers and some of them were really mean. That's the other big turn around I've seen with her, is when she went into this DBT program last May, she quit having to have a guy all the time, no matter who it was, just to love her. Now she can love herself and start making better choices, be more selective. Actually she hasn't gone out with anyone since she started this program and again that tells me her self-worth has improved immeasurably.

I always said to the kids, when they were going through adolescence, "Just get through there without any permanent damage." In this case, permanent damage is ruining your body. A lot of these girls end up with osteoporosis, they end up with heart damage, they can't have children, even after they recover, they've done permanent damage.

Hailey: Their eyebrows fall out, like mine.

Sue: My daughter was at the Unit one day when a girl found out she'd ruined her reproductive system and she would never be able to have kids. She was about your age, Hailey. It was very sad.

Hailey: That happens all the time with anorexia.

Val: So that's what I always hoped for my kids- no permanent damage. There's a few scars [from self-harm], but you know what? We all have them. I have them on inside, some people have them on the outside. Thank God she didn't end up with any of those guys.

• Hope

Hailey: I have hope now, but I don't feel I HAD any hope. (*Speaking to her mom*) I feel like you guys were the ones who had hope and faith in me. And that was the only reason I got through it. I don't think I had any hope then.

Val: Do you feel hope for your future?

Hailey: Right now, school gives me hope. I can't believe I got my diploma with all that stuff going on. I essentially did high school by myself at home. And I got into one of the most prestigious universities in western Canada and I feel like, "I can do it." Hopefully I can keep doing it. What it's called in DBT is "Building Mastery", which is just pretty much building up the qualities that make you feel like a person that's good for the world, with a life worth living, and for me, that's school. Because I'm going to be a psych nurse. I've learned that psychiatry really interests me.

Val: You have so much to offer.

Hailey: If I was on the Eating Disorder Unit [as a nurse], I know I would be really caring.

Sue: Is another gift of this illness compassion and understanding? Not on a text book level, but on an experiential level.

Hailey: Exactly. You can see the difference. Even on the Unit, if you look at Dr. O and Dr. P. She's experienced it and he hasn't and you can see the difference in the doctors. She's so amazing. She inspired me to be a psych nurse too.

Val: Dr. O never gives up.

Hailey: Nope, she's never given up on me. Never.

Val: She just keeps at it.

Hailey: She's like my second Mom, for sure.

Sue: What gave you hope, Val, as a parent?

Val: Nothing gave me hope when I was in it. No, I felt completely hopeless. Completely hopeless. And unfortunately, her moods were my moods. We were so inter-connected and there was real codependency, which wasn't good for her and wasn't good for me. And even still, when she's not doing well, I'm not doing well and when she's doing good, I'm doing good. We have interconnectedness. We just do. And that's just the way it is.

Hailey: And it's not your fault either. It started out because I had separation anxiety when I was very, very young and persisted until... it still does. So because of my separation anxiety, we became really close and it damaged us, I guess.

Val: Yeah, it did. It is so hard being responsible or making yourself feel like you are wholly responsible for another human being. That is so hard. They are standing in the middle of the railroad tracks and the train is coming straight for them and you're screaming and you're screaming, *"Get off, get off, get off!!"*

I guess through it all, the only thing that made me feel hopeful is she was so smart, intellectually. Even when she wasn't eating and couldn't think straight, I still believed she was too smart to... fill in the blank. 'She's too smart to: kill herself. She's too smart to: get pregnant with that guy. She's too smart to: let this carry on.' I had no hope, but I had faith in her abilities. I thought, 'She's too smart, she's too smart, she's too smart. Eventually she's going to figure it out.' And she has.

I opened a fortune cookie. I stuck it on my mirror and when things are really, really bad... here it is (*reading*): "Faith is knowing there is an ocean, when you can only see the stream."

It's faith, it's really not hope because, to me, faith is deeper than hope. Faith is a belief that she'll get there.

I mean there are still days. When she's having a bad day, she's so hard on herself, but she's working on that in the DBT: to be kind to herself, and not to bully herself.

Hailey: There are honestly more good days than bad days.

Val: Oh yeah, it's way better and she's so much easier to get along with and to live with and to be with and do things with. Because she's so nice. I forgot that she's actually a nice person. I did. For a little while, I forgot. We had our moments, where our frustration levels were huge.

• Which emotions did you feel?

Hailey: Shame and guilt, for sure. 100%. In my DBT, the biggest emotion problem right now is the shame. Everything else I've learned to deal with, but the shame is so habitual, it's so hard to get rid of. Sadness was bad, but shame was the worst.

Val: You had a lot of anger too, when you were restricting.

Hailey: That was irritability, that wasn't anger. It's just feeling bad and not enough, like you're doing something to hurt someone. Your presence is making someone else's life miserable.

Val: You have to be so vulnerable to overcome shame. There is a lot of [the eating disorder] that's secret.

As a parent, regret was the biggest one. I wanted to take the way I raised my kids, like an *Etch-A-Sketch* and just redo it all. I wanted to start all over again. I wanted to have the book on validation. I wanted to be older; I was young when I had my kids. I wanted to be smarter, I wanted a husband that worked in town. It's just regret. You just regret the whole way you did it. I overprotected her—that's part of my regret—because I didn't want her to get hurt. Probably because I was really wild kid as a teenager and I didn't want her to be exposed to any of that. But they are, anyway. You just feel so incapable. You kind of feel like a loser. Where did I screw up? Everyone else's kid is eating supper!

Sue: This experience has made me doubt myself as a parent, question my choices, it's very discombobulating.

Val: Oh, I was just going to say that word: discombobulating. It is. You're on a *Tilt-a-whirl*. I thought if you just loved them to pieces, you'd be okay. Just love them so much and give them everything you could and don't let them fall, or struggle, or feel pain, or feel anxiety or feel depression. Make it all better. Which did my kids absolutely no good. I blew it in that respect.

• How would you describe your life now?

Hailey: It was really bad, but honestly right now life is so much better. It really it is. You actually have the capability of being happy, which you don't when you are starving. Nothing can make you happy, at that point. It's really hard to understand when you are sick: how could gaining weight make me happy? But it really does.

Val: I never believed it when they said, "She won't be depressed anymore when she's eating properly." I didn't believe it.

Hailey: I didn't believe it either. I was diagnosed with major depression.

Val: It was major starvation they should have diagnosed her with. And since she's eating properly, she's happier. You're joking around. You're good to yourself.

Hailey: You just need to know your parents are going to be there, and support you and love you, no matter what.

Sue: If you had to summarize your journey in one sentence, what would it be?

Hailey: I don't know how to put it in a sentence. That's so hard. It's too big.

Val: "We have been through a hurricane and we're rebuilding and we're all still alive."

Hailey: I just feel like I had a demon inside me, and now I'm fighting it and it's leaving me alone.

Val: You're winning.

Hailey: Exactly. That's how I feel about this thing: it's a demon. For sure.

Val: If I think back over the stuff we went through, I can't believe it. I can't even believe it.

Sue: I have learned that I can handle more than I ever thought possible.

Hailey: Yeah, I learned that too about myself.

Val: Because you have to. You're on. Right? You're not allowed to curl up in bed and stay there. You're not allowed to fall into the abyss. You're not allowed to. If you really want to be there for your kid, that's not an option.

Hailey: You know what it's like? It's like the exact same thing they say people that are trying to quit smoking, they say: "Never Quit Quitting." That's the biggest thing. I tell my friend [who has an eating disorder] that every day: "Just don't stop trying. Keep trying to make this go away. Keep trying to quit this disorder."

"Half of those who struggle with eating disorders are also involved in drug or alcohol abuse, compared to 9% of public who abuse substances. Best practice today is to treat the conditions simultaneously."

www.elementsbehaviouralhealth.com/

eating-disorders/eating-disorders-chemical dependency

Patients who have both eating disorders and substance abuse problems require longer hospitalization and treatment. They are at a higher risk for other behaviours characterised by poor impulse control [like shoplifting] and increased risk of self-injury or suicide.

— *The Practice Guideline for the Treatment of Patients with Eating Disorders*, Third Edition, 2006, American Psychiatric Association

ORIGINAL ART: PARRY WYMINGA SCOTT, AGE 13

Siblings

Over the past year, Hannah has had frightening panic attacks, during which she would cry inconsolably, sometimes pulling at her hair or clawing at her skin. I would try to reach her, but her eyes were flat and lifeless, blinded by emotions too big for her tiny body to bear. It was horrifying to watch and, acting on instinct, I would wrap her in a blanket and hold her tight. In part I did this to keep her from hurting herself, but mostly I wanted to shield her against the darkness that seemed to threaten to swallow her whole. Often, the swaddling seemed to work and she would eventually settle, exhausted, and fall asleep.

Our son, Josh hated being in the house when these attacks happened. He began distancing himself from behaviours that he found upsetting, scary and, at times, infuriating by spending more and more time out of the house and less time around Hannah. A huge wedge began to develop between them. I felt like I was barely keeping my head above water and there wasn't much energy left for him. I know Josh often felt ignored.

One evening, Hannah had a panic attack that I couldn't quell. I was utterly out of ideas, so I asked her, "What do you need?" She said one word: "Josh". He had just been picked up by a carload of friends to go out for an evening of fun. I wasn't sure what he would say when I called him, but he simply told his friends: "My sister needs me."

Within minutes, he entered Hannah's bedroom and sat on her bed, as she lay curled up in a ball. He gave her an awkward side hug and said a few comforting words. I left the room, choking back the tears.

Hannah asked that I include this story in the book. For her, it was a turning point in her recovery. Up until that day, she feared that her relationship with him would be destroyed by her illness and the thought of losing him was terrifying. From that moment on, however, their bond has been unbreakable and Hannah considers him to be the unsung hero in her recovery.

Lauren

Age at interview: 21
Age of onset: 16
Treatment: at home, with regular appointments

"Oh, the guilt. It was so heavy."

"Hope is knowing where you're at, isn't where you're
 supposed to be."

"I still have to say it (to myself):
You're good enough. You're good enough.
You're good enough."

• Overview

Starting in Grade 10, whenever I would feel upset, I would eat food, that's
how I would numb and then I started gaining weight. In about Grade 12,
I decided I wanted to lose weight, so I went on *Weight Watchers* and it was
good. I lost "X" pounds and then I just got obsessed. I would lie about my
height and weight, so I could lose even more weight. And I would lie to my
parents about what I was eating. You're supposed to have like 25 points so
I would cut it down to 12 points a day. But everyone was like, "You are on
Weight Watchers. Good job, keep it up."

When I started losing weight was when my dad, I think, kind of realized
his mistakes when I was growing up. So, coincidence—just the way the

timing worked out—when I started losing weight was when he started to say he loved me, telling me I was beautiful and hugging me and stuff like that. And I also got a boyfriend who was really sweet and loved me. Everything started working for me as I was losing this weight, so in my head it was cemented that your weight is your happiness. Your weight is your worth.

I got really skinny.

Then everyone started to notice. "You are too skinny. You need to stop this *Weight Watchers*." And I'm like No! I need to lose another X pounds. I need to lose this and this (*indicating parts of her body*) even though bones were sticking out. So then people were on my case: "You need to eat more, you need to eat more, this isn't healthy."

So I started eating more, but I couldn't do it. So then I began throwing up and that became an everyday occurrence. Four times a day, that's all I did. Everything revolved around it. If I was going to dinner that night, I would plan all day what I was going to eat, how I would throw it up, where I was going to store my toothbrush, how I would tie my hair up so I wouldn't mess it up. That was my entire day, that was it. I ended my relationship with my boyfriend; I didn't care about him anymore. I just became numb. I was like a vegetable.

For almost two years, I was very bulimic. That was all I had in my life, really. All I cared about. I tried to quit. I'd go up and down. Up and down. I'd get these moments where I'd be at the bottom and I'd think: 'You need to get out, claw your way out this hole. This is it. I'm never going to throw up again. This is it. This is the last time. I need to get better. You can do it.'

And then two days later, I'd be back in it. I'd be up and down, up and down. And finally I got so low I was like, 'I need to tell my parents. I need to tell them exactly when I do it. I need to tell them exactly what my triggers are.' I basically exposed everything and that was really hard, because that was honestly my life. My life revolved around it, so I couldn't have my life, really. So I told them: "If you see me eating these types of food, I will throw them up. When I have showers, that is when I'm throwing up, so you need to check on me." I told them everything. A couple of days later, I hated myself 'cuz all I wanted was to go back to that, my comfort, and I couldn't because I had exposed everything. So I almost got worse then: I started doing it in parking lots, in back alleys, in bags... Oh, it was terrible. I would go to my friend's house and do it there.

And they wanted me to go see a doctor and I didn't want to go: "I can do it on my own, I can do it on my own." Eventually I got in to see Dr. O and she wanted me to go into the day program but I didn't want to. It was kind of slow. It was like every time I tried to quit and failed, I got even further down. I got to the point where I didn't even want to try quitting anymore, because I thought I'm just going to fail and to hate myself. I felt more and more pathetic every time. So that was probably the hardest part emotionally: the failure, the repeating failure, not being able to do it.

My identity changed from: I'm a girl who plays soccer. I'm a Christian girl who sings and struggles with bulimia and it transitioned to: I'm a bulimic. That's who I am. That's what I am. I accepted that. I went even further down because it became Me. My identity.

When I was really sick, nothing made me happy. I would come home to Holly, she'd would be wagging her tail and I would walk right past her. I didn't care. I didn't care about anything. My best friend moved to Nova Scotia and I was just numb. Didn't care. Didn't cry. Nothing. I stopped singing. I didn't ever want to. I was like a zombie. It was weird. When I started taking *Prozac*, I started noticing genuine happiness coming back into my life. Like coming home and having so much joy seeing my dog. I never had that for years.

I went on a mission trip [with a church] to downtown Los Angeles. It's funny how it worked. The lead guy for the camps was saying, "You should come" and I'm like, "There's no way, I can't afford that. I'm saving money for Thailand, for University, there's no way I can do that." I am in my room one time and I had this flashback to this financial course I did with my parents. I used to keep envelopes of money in my underwear drawer. I had this envelope that said 'Shopping' and envelope that said "Gas Money". And I'm remembering.... I don't think I used those envelopes. I looked and

I had this "Mission Trips" envelope that had $750 in it that I'd forgotten about. But still, this trip is going to cost $2000, so I still can't afford it. I talk to the director and he says, "We're not flying, we're driving, it's only $700." So it was like a smack in the face from God that I should go. And that was scary because He knew. Because He knew about me and my struggles.

So I went.

This one night everyone was opening up. I didn't want to say I had an eating disorder because I always want to be a perfect person, dress perfectly, look perfect, to be the perfect role model and so to be open about this was absolutely terrifying. I was shaking but I said, "I'm struggling with an addiction" and that's kind of where I left it and they prayed with me and I said, "God, I need to put this on you, because I can't do it myself. I've been trying."

Ultimately, I stopped making it about me, stopped making it about my strength, because if I'm relying on me and what I can do, I hated myself so much, that wouldn't work. So I transitioned it: it's not about me. That really helped a lot.

So I stopped throwing up then and I haven't thrown up since then. It hasn't been easy. I transitioned. I would binge and then I would starve myself for five days. So it's not like I got better. I just knocked one thing off that I don't worry about now. So that's where the recovery from bulimia came in, but still my eating wasn't right.

Even now, I still struggle. If I'm feeling anxious, I binge, and then I spend three days hating myself. If I get caught up in how many calories I've eaten, I get so upset and it's such a weight on my shoulders. But I'm really trying to back up and look at a week rather than the day. Like: 'You used to puke four times a day for a whole week straight and now you binged maybe once this week. That's amazing!' And yeah maybe my pants are a little bit tight, but I just have to consciously tell myself that's not who I am anymore.

• How would you define recovery?

Recovery is... um... I dunno... it was making something more important in my life than being perfect. I had to shift my priorities. Because before, honestly, all I cared about was being thin, getting attention from guys, being hunted by guys. That was all I cared about. That was my worth and I had to stop and I had to shift what was important to me. And it was hard, of course, but I realized I can't start my life while I'm doing this. I value a family, going to school, having a good career and there was no way I could go to school while I had my eating disorder. There was no way. Recovery is wanting a future.

Recovery is letting go of the idea of being perfect. It's okay. You are good enough. I still have to say it ten times over in my head: You're good enough. You're good enough. You're good enough. You're good enough....

I think a gift I've gotten from this experience is I'm very empathetic. I see young girls that are wearing short skirts and people are like "Ugh! Gross!" and I just want to hold them in my arms and tell them they are so beautiful. It makes me cry thinking of it. I have such a heart for people who don't feel good enough, who didn't get the attention they want. I've been working at summer camps and I get no greater satisfaction than making these girls feel so beautiful. I think that's a gift I've gotten from this. That's made me want to be a junior high school counsellor, 'cuz there are so many people who don't have what they need to become healthy, successful people. They don't have the love.

• What have you learned about yourself?

I've learned that moving targets are toxic. For me growing up, it was like, "Oh Dad, I got 85% on this test." "Oh? What happened to the 15%?" Nothing was ever good enough. I just find it so important to consciously say: "Good job, you reached it, you did it, you're wonderful." That's so important. I look at parents that are pushing their kids to be better and better and better and the kids never get the satisfaction of being good enough.

I've learned too that I'm worthy of getting help, I guess. That I'm not an inconvenience. The whole reason I didn't tell my family at first, 'cuz I've always felt like a burden. If I tell them that I need help, they were going to have to inconvenience themselves, shift their lives. And it made me feel so guilty.

Oh, so guilty.

I remember even at the beginning, they would call me, "Lauren, are you OK?"—I know my dad is always so busy at work—"Lauren, are doing alright?" I would get so angry at myself. Don't worry about me. I hated that they were tweaking their lives to accommodate me. I felt so weak and pathetic, that I have been raised in a home where I'm loved, I'm so blessed, and I still managed to be so screwed up. Oh, the guilt. It was so heavy.

I tried so hard to be perfect. So people would be, "Wow, you are so succesful. You're so happy all the time. You're so sweet." Everyone had me up on this pedestal. And I remember my auntie saying, "I want my daughter to end up just like you. You are such a role model for my daughter." And I just wanted to throw up. I just wanted to scream, "Just get her away from me! Don't get her anything like me! I don't want anyone to have to end up like me." I have parents who love me and yeah it hasn't been perfect, but no one's life is perfect. There's people that have it way harder than me, that are better than me, that was how I looked at it. The guilt was the hardest thing to get over.

I'm still learning. I'm still trying to teach myself: I'm worthy of help. I'm worthy of being healthy. And I'm learning to accept help. I'm learning my parents don't find me an inconvenience. They love me and I need to accept that.

• Feelings

Shame is at the root of it. It's such a cycle, you try to quit, and you fail and you have all this shame and you're like, 'I don't know what to do with this feeling. Why don't I just binge and purge again? That will fix it!' And then you feel guilty about it. There's just so much shame. I feel so much shame. I have the most wonderful mom I could ever ask for and I turned out so twisted and stuff.

Even my mom being a good mom, I would twist that into making me feel terrible: "You're never going to be as good a mom as your mom. She's so good. You can't do that."

I'm trying to get past this, but there so much guilt and shame. So much. My brothers are all successful and smart and, at the beginning, I was like, "Why did I screw up? Why couldn't I...? Why was I the weak one?" That's why I always felt so guilty about it. And I'm seeing a counsellor about it and he told me, "You're not the weak one, you just dealt with it in a different way." He went through all my brothers and said, "This is how he dealt with it. This is how they dealt with it." And it just made me feel like I'm not alone and I'm not weak and I'm not pathetic.

• Overcoming setbacks

A habit I had, when I would screw up, I would lock myself in my room and sleep and be depressed and feel so terrible. One thing my parents helped me with, when I was feeling like that, they would say, "You are not going to bed. Let's go. Put on your boots, we're going outside. You gotta get distracted." They forced me. I was angry at first, but when I got back [from the walk], I was really grateful. When your world is your eating disorder— seriously, that was my world—when you fail in that, it's not just a screw up. It's your entire being. It's your entire worth.

I remember my head telling me these things: "You're beautiful. You're good enough." But I didn't feel it. Your heart doesn't feel it. Every day, I would write things, things I loved about myself. It slowly creeps into your heart. It's hard work. Realizing there's an end goal, there are bigger things, there's so much to life.

Even my sister-in-law, she was trying to quit drinking *Coke*—she's addicted to drinking cans of *Coke*—she went three months without having a *Coke* and then she had a *Coke* and she said, "It's like I'm back at square one, it's like I'm starting over." And I had this huge feeling: "You're not! You are not back at square one! You think of the progress you have made. You had a slip up. Get back on track."

That was huge for me: To look at all the progress I've made, get back on track, keep going. Look at how much I've accomplished. Recently, I gained X pounds, this was the hardest thing, telling myself: "You know what, Lauren? If you gain X, 2X pounds, it's still better than being skinny and sick." I'd rather be healthy in whatever body shape than "perfect" and so sick and not being able to experience the good things in life.

• Who helped you through?

My mom. I just remember lying on that couch there, bawling, saying, "Mom, this is going to be me for the rest of my life and I'm not going to get out of this. I can't." I'd try and try and try. I just felt like I just was falling back in the hole and was starting over again. But every day is a new day. You wake up and reset your mind. It's a new day.

My parents helped a lot. I had calendars with check marks or Xs [to keep track of good days], so I was accountable. There were tons and tons of things. I told my friends. A lot of help. But still, my darkest times, I was pretty alone because I didn't want to burden anyone. I was very good at hiding it. I think I did a lot of it on my own.

My faith. Reading verses about my identity gave me a new perspective: that I'm not measured by what I do, or how good I am at something or my failures. That's not me. I am made beautiful, exactly as God wants me to be.

• What gave you hope?

Good days. Hope was even little stupid things: I would put two crackers in my soup I'd be, "OK!!" Little things like, that, that are so, so miniscule, it's just a little step, but you think: "I can do this. I can eat like a normal person." Just little steps at a time and celebrating those little things. I ordered a chocolate milk one time. Oh my gosh, it was huge. I told my friend, she was crying, "Oh my god! You ordered a chocolate milk. This is so huge!!" Just celebrating the little accomplishments, because I never felt good enough. But if you celebrate every little thing you do, you build up hope.

Hope was huge. If I didn't have it, why quit? Why stop? If I didn't think I could do it, if I didn't think I could get out of it? Waste of my time, waste of my tears. I could go back to being a numb vegetable that didn't feel anything. If I didn't have hope, there's no way I'd get better. I'd probably be dead.

Hope is knowing that where you're at, isn't where you're supposed to be. There is so much more. I love kids and I love family and I knew, where I was, there was no way I could do that. And so in my head, I knew: 'This isn't where it ends, this isn't me. I just have to get past this.' I knew there was so much more to life and I just needed to work my butt off, and cry and swear and get through it.

Sue: You've already mentioned telling your family the truth and admitting you had a problem on the mission trip in Los Angeles, where there other turning points?

Yeah, those were definitely two huge ones. I think another turning point, this isn't as huge, but I gained a lot of weight 'cuz still I didn't know how to deal with my emotions, so I dealt with it with food but I just stopped puking it up. And so I was gaining weight and I hated myself. Oh my gosh, I hated myself but I knew I couldn't puke even one time, because I would just spiral down. I knew I couldn't do it. So I'm gaining weight, gaining weight, hating myself, just feeling so disgusting and pathetic and this, um, this guy I've liked for years, asked me to be his girlfriend when I was the biggest I've ever been. It was a realisation: It's not about the number on the scale.

Turning points keep happening. So I had a physics exam coming up, couple of weeks ago and I didn't feel prepared, and I was stressing out and I just started to hyperventilating. My head was coming outside my body and I was going, "Lauren, relax, it's just an exam. Like who cares?" But my body... I was sweating. I think I was having an anxiety attack—I believe—I've never had one before.

And then my dad came into my room. He had his big boss over for dinner and I was having a panic attack in my room. And I was freaking out, because I'm supposed to be the perfect, perfect daughter that is polite and smiling and just making my dad feel very accomplished in front of this man he looks up to. And so, Dad comes into my room and spends twenty minutes in my room with me and the whole time, I'm like, "What are you doing? You need to get out there. Don't worry about me." And he comes and he sits there and he's like, "Lauren, what is the worst thing that could happen tomorrow for your exam?" I said, "I could get a zero." And he said, "Yeah, and then, we pick up our socks, we get you a tutor." And he said, "It's okay to fail." And to hear that from him, it was the most beautiful thing. That's not how he raised me! It was definitely not okay to fail. There's no way! So hearing my dad contradicting everything he ever put in my head... it was huge. It put me at ease, hearing it from him.

• Life now

I still have far to go, but I look back to a year ago and—oh wow—Life is so beautiful. Life now is really great. Of course, no one's life is perfect. You have your days. But life is beautiful. There's just so much more to life than what it was. I have so much more joy. I do still struggle. I feel guilty— I'm huge with the guilt (*laughs*). I have these voices, "You think you're better, but you're relying on meds to get better. You are weak." I have these little lies in my head, but, no, I have to be very proud of myself for how far I've come. I definitely have more strength in myself now. I can accomplish things in life, like becoming a school counsellor. I can be so successful and I will be a good mom.

It's one step at a time, you fall, but you get back up. It's okay to fail. Life is wonderful. What I'm good at, I'm really good at. Definitely. You just get a whole new outlook on yourself and life.

Sue: This is such a gift to me, and my daughter, to know that recovery is possible. Because when you are in it, it's just feels so far away, beyond your grasp. But to know that real people go through this and struggle with it, just as much as you have struggled with it, and come out the other side; to hear you say you feel joy again and that life is beautiful... this is such a gift. To see you, to talk with you, is like a drink of water in the middle of the desert. Thank you. So much.

"Specific pressures and values concerning weight and shape vary among different cultures. The quest for beauty and acceptance in accordance with the stereotypes women perceive in contemporary media is leading increasing number of women around the world to develop attitudes and eating behaviours associated with eating disorders. Despite initally higher prevalence rates of this phenomenon in Western and postindustrial societies, disordered eating behaviours now appear to be globally distributed."

— *The Practice Guideline for the Treatment of Patients with Eating Disorders*, Third Edition, 2006, American Psychiatric Association

ORIGINAL ART: PARRY WYMINGA SCOTT, AGE 13

Rena (Lauren's mom)

"Who do we contact? And where do you go?"

"Through all this, Lauren will be able to help others."

"I think 'recovery' is almost a misnomer."

Rena: I think first of all, the acknowledgement that there's a problem [is hard]. The first year or so, I thought it was just a passing thing. Hers was a more gradual shift. It was several months, she threw up and then it was quite a while before she threw up again. When I was 18, 19, 20, I also, you know, had some bulimic episodes as well, but I never got addicted to it. I was in that mind set too, 'OK, well, it will pass.'

But it wasn't until she shared it with us—I can't remember how old she was even, maybe 18—when she told us it was a serious situation. That was like: Wow!! It hits you between the eyes. And then the scariness of it: 'Kay, where do we go? How do we embark on this journey to wellness? Who do we contact? And where do you go? What is the best way of attacking it? There were other people who had maybe gone through it themselves, or kids [who had] gone through it, but not to the extent that Lauren was struggling. So nobody had really been where we were.

I phoned a friend of mine who is a public health nurse and she put me in touch with another public health nurse who had done a lot of work with eating disorders. Then she referred me to a dietician and a psychiatrist [Dr. O]. The public health nurse that I spoke said, "Dr. O wants to nip things in the bud, sooner rather than later." And that was one of the things she recommended about using her. That's when I went to the GP and I asked for referrals to these people and she didn't want to do this. She said, "Oh well, we do it this way." AHH!..I had just spoken with the experts. I felt like she wasn't willing to work with us at all and that was extremely frustrating because we were quite concerned. Lauren didn't want to go to our regular GP, because she was embarrassed, so this GP wasn't very familiar with us, so that was one of the issues.

The GP finally succumbed. So when Lauren finally got into see the psychiatrist, and the dietician and she started getting some help—the right resources, the right help—that was relieving. However, it seemed like it wasn't happening fast enough. And then she started seeing this Christian psychologist about a year ago and he's been a huge benefit to her as well, having that kind of support too. It's a very, very, very slow process and it still is, because we're still not out of it. There have definitely been improvements. We're climbing the hill, we're getting there, but we're still on the path. That was kind of frustrating, but, I guess, you just appreciate the... um... small... um... successes along the way.

It's an addiction and so it is something that Lauren's psychologist said that she will always deal with, she will always struggle with. And so recovery is the ability not to succumb to the addictive leanings, I guess. Acceptance. It's accepting that this is the new norm; this is what life is. I think 'recovery' is almost a misnomer. I don't know that you recover because you can never go back to the way it was.

Sue: What word would you use to describe it?

Rena: It's almost acceptance, but it's got to be a positive acceptance. Adaptation?

Sue: Transformation?

Rena: Yeah, transformation would be a good word. That would be a good word.

Sue: Like a caterpillar to butterfly?

Rena: Yeah, huge change, but it's slow.

The way I view life, God brings things into our lives, experiences, that enable us to benefit others. So through all this, Lauren will be able to help others. When people go through loss, they can always assist others who aren't as far down the path as they are. I'm excited to think about Lauren going into counselling. She wants to be a junior high or high school counsellor, and she'll be able to pick up on this stuff. She'll recognize where the girls are at—boys, as well—but more so girls.

The gift for me? Going through this is enhancing my experience as a nurse, my view of wellness. Also, recognizing my own frailties or whatever, my own issues, that maybe I should have been more protective [of Lauren]. That's one thing. I don't know if that's a gift, or a self-realization, a learning, self-awareness? Maybe more of an awareness of what's going on around me. I can see things in other relationships, maybe family relationships, cautionary things, like: 'Be careful what you say to your daughter. Be careful how you respond.' Not everybody in the extended family knows about Lauren's situation, so I don't have the ability to say things now that I might otherwise. Down the road, I suppose, that will come too.

My husband grew up with a very authoritarian family; everything was very rigid. You do this and you do that. This is the right way and 'Don't talk back' and this kind of stuff. I know that he didn't want to replicate that environment in our family, but, as much as he loves our kids, some of that stuff carried over. I don't want him to come across as the bad guy—he's not at all—but there's been a change in my husband. He began to treat her with kid gloves. He was much more aware of where she was at, psychologically, and that was good, because he was no longer putting the pressure on her that she had before. I think he just didn't know how to raise a daughter. This is the way you raise the three boys, and this is what will work for her.

• What emotions did you experience?

Rena: I don't know… it was like the sense in my stomach, it just kept hitting me in my stomach. It was like: "*Uughhhh!*" [I felt] sadness for Lauren, just feeling empathy, just wishing I could help her and take it away.

"Oh no, it's happening again. It's happening again!"

Sue: Watching your child suffer, knowing how horrible they feel and being utterly powerless to do anything about it, that is so painful as a parent.

Rena (*about Lauren*): "You have so much going for you, why don't you see it?"

Sue: But you can't make them see themselves through your eyes. It is their journey. Accepting that has been so hard for me. What has been the hardest part for you?

Rena: I mean beyond the emotional stuff, I think just trying to monitor her eating, especially when she asked for it: "Mom, watch me. Make sure that I'm doing this. Make sure I'm doing that." And just the day-to-day grind. I'd ask her: "Are you OK?" And she'd say, "Oh, you just caught me. That's good, thank you." Or "No, thanks, I'm fine. I'm in a good space." It doesn't stop. You have to keep on monitoring. Now, she's not doing the bulimic stuff anymore, just bingeing, and that's absolutely awesome. Huge, huge steps!

When the bulimia stopped, she'd say, "OK, it's been a month, it's been six months, it's been a year." That was just, "Ahhh! Thank you, God."

Because before [when she was bulimic], her hair stylist was saying, "What's the matter with your hair? It's in really rough shape." But Lauren wasn't going to tell her what the problem was. Her periods had stopped, all that typical stuff. Thankfully, she's come out of that part. So we're just dealing with the bingeing and just trying to identify the triggers. All the stress at school is a huge trigger, so at exam time or other stressful times, we know to watch out. So we text: 'How are you doing?' Or phone: "What are your eating plans?" It's becoming much more defined and predictable.

Sue: What helped you through the dark times?

Rena: Knowing that she had good support. When she started to see Dr. Ostolosky, when she got that connection, it was like, 'Okay, she's in good hands now.' I believed in what Dr. Ostolosky could do with her and help her, I think that was it. I think probably just a lot of prayer too.

We prayed a lot. Still do.

• How did you deal with setbacks?

Rena: I think recognizing that we're still on the forward path, that she has made progress. Don't focus on the little missteps. Keep on going. I think looking at the big picture and realizing: 'Look how far we've come.' And believing. You hold onto the hope that she's going to make it out, to a healthy place. Just having hope.

I think seeing the good that is going to come out of this [gives me hope], knowing that these difficulties are going to be used in a positive way. When Lauren made her life plans and goals—to go ahead with her education—that would be another one, knowing that she had those plans [was hopeful].

I think hope is the ability to see that something is going to be different down the road. More positive. You're not stuck in the moment. That they will be better, that they will change, they will improve.

• Life now

The key to staying well is identifying the triggers, being open and acknowledging it. It's still a journey, for us, but it's getting easier, because Lauren is much more open about her struggles, so we can work with it. She's more mature, so it's getting easier. What do they say in the AADAC program? "One day at a time."

And I'm very excited about where Lauren is going to be down the road, to help others. It's exactly what you are doing right now [with the book]. You are taking this experience and you're utilizing this to assist others. Someday, your daughter, too, will be able to help somebody else down the road because of all the things she's gone through. She will save someone's life. And I believe that about Lauren, too.

Sue: Is there anything else you'd like to add?

Rena: Have you ever heard of Dietrich Bonhoeffer? He was a German theologian, a very, very intelligent man. He was one of the people that was standing up against Nazism, and he was put in the prison camps. Then later they found out he was involved in an attempt to assasinate Hitler and he was executed two weeks before the end of the second World War. He was an amazing guy. In the prison camps, everybody always spoke so highly of him because he was always so kind to everybody, including his captors. Everybody looked up to him. But he wrote a poem about how, on the outside, everyone sees one thing, but who am I really? He was going through all these struggles, but nobody ever knew. It was a very poignant poem, so I framed it for Lauren and gave it to her.

Who am I? They often tell me
I stepped from my cell's confinement
Calmly, cheerfully, firmly,
Like a Squire from his country house.

Who am I? They often tell me
I used to speak to my wardens
Freely and friendly and clearly,
As though it were mine to command.

Who am I? They also tell me
I bore the days of misfortune
Equably, smilingly, proudly,
like one accustomed to win.

Am I then really that which other men tell of?
Or am I only what I myself know of myself?
Restless and longing and sick, like a bird in a cage,
Struggling for breath, as though hands were compressing my throat,
Yearning for colors, for flowers, for the voices of birds,
Thirsting for words of kindness, for neighborliness,
Tossing in expectations of great events,
Powerlessly trembling for friends at an infinite distance,
Weary and empty at praying, at thinking, at making,
Faint, and ready to say farewell to it all.

Who am I? This or the Other?
Am I one person today and tomorrow another?
Am I both at once? A hypocrite before others,
And before myself a contemptible woebegone weakling?
Or is something within me still like a beaten army
Fleeing in disorder from victory already achieved?
Who am I? They mock me, these lonely questions of mine.
Whoever I am, Thou knowest, O God, I am thine!

Acceptance

I met a woman whose daughter had been in the grips of anorexia for four years. Because her daughter was an adult when the illness manifested, she and her husband felt powerless to compel her to seek treatment. We began exchanging emails and her anguish and exhaustion were obvious. Her husband had suggested that perhaps they should just accept that their daughter would live with them forever and would never be able to function independently. It made me wonder about the role of acceptance in this illness, so I wrote the following to her in my next email:

I will accept that you have an eating disorder. I will accept that this illness causes you to lash out in ways that I find painful. I will accept that it will take time for you to recover, that recovery will not be a straight line, nor will it return us to the life we knew before you got sick. I will accept that change is needed and some of that change will be found in me,

but:

I will not accept that this is all your life can be. I will not accept that you are doomed to live a life of fear and self-loathing. I will not accept this diminished version of you as all you will ever be.
I will not stand by and let you die.

PHOTO: JENNY HAWKINS

Sarah

Age of onset: 16
Age at interview: 23

"If I was going to have an eating disorder, I was going to be
the best one with it."

"It's pretty bad when you get banned from the hospital."

"They loved me until I was able to love myself."

Sarah: I agreed to do this [interview] because, going through what I went through and being on the other side, I feel it's very important to give back and help others struggling. I feel too, the people who do get better, don't go back. I haven't been up there [4F4], because I just can't. I don't want to. Yet. So [when you are sick] you kind of feel like there are no success stories. You feel that everyone must stay sick. I think if there would've been something like this [book] available when I was going through it, it would have helped a lot and the same with my family, too. They had no idea about anything. And parents going through it, don't know what to do.

• Overview

Growing up, I always had very low self-esteem and always hated myself quite a bit. I was searching out anything to be someone else, in a kind of way. It started not in the average way. I've never made myself throw up, I just could—it was mental, I think—one day, I just threw up. I was feeling really full and I just threw up and something went off in my head: I feel better! It was kind of weird. Everything happened really quickly; I started not keeping any food down. Nobody knew what was going on. I didn't know what was going on. I was losing a lot of weight—like a lot of weight—really quickly. As soon as I started losing all that weight, it took over. That became my main focus: just obsessing about not eating or if I was going to eat, how I was going to throw it up. It just became crazy.

So I was actually put into the Stollery [Children's Hospital] because they thought something was wrong with my digestion or acid reflux or something like that. When I was there, they couldn't find anything so they said, "We're going to go see a doctor so that you can talk about the stress of being in the hospital." Which was kind of a trick 'cuz they brought me to 4F4 [the Eating Disorder Unit]. And I walked in... I just remember it being the scariest place ever. There was all these really skinny girls, wrapped in blankets, with tubes up their nose and I'm like 'Where am I?'

And I went in and saw Dr. P and told him kind of what was going on and he asked me one question: "If you could gain back all the weight that you lost, would you?" and I said, "No, obviously not." And from there, he said, "Well, you have an eating disorder." I was like, "OK, I don't believe that. But whatever." I was furious because I'd been tricked.

So I went back to my room in the Stollery and I didn't even want to tell my brother or my mom what had just happened, so I kept it a secret. I met with the dietician before I left and she gave me meal plans to try and do it on my own. I think it was like three weeks. I came back. "No, I can't eat anything. It's not working."

And so I was admitted. I was 16, I believe.

I came as an outpatient for the first 6 months. By that point, I was so small that my brain wasn't really working that well and I became very, very sneaky. It just kind of grabbed hold—if I was going to have an eating disorder, I was going to be the best one with it. I was outpatient, but I didn't have a Close Band on [a coloured ID wrist band that limits permission to leave the locked unit]. Somehow I befriended the guard and he just thought I was a visitor, so after every single meal, I would sneak off and throw up, like it was nothing. For months. So my meal plan calories were getting more and more and more because I wasn't gaining any weight. So the more my calories went up, the more I had to sneak off until... until I was busted and that's when I was admitted as an inpatient. That just started a whole new journey.

I was put on all these prescription medications, like fourteen of them, and I didn't know what any of them were. I didn't want to be there. I didn't understand why I was there and I was surrounding myself with people who didn't want to be there and didn't want to get help. So we spent our day talking about how much we hated our bodies and how we were going to lose weight. I was in and out, and in and out, and in and out of there.

I was probably an inpatient... I don't even know... ten or twelve times in four years. I dropped out of school at 16. I was just in the hospital. I'd go in there for four months until I hit my [target] weight, leave and lose the weight as fast as I could to go back. It was all I knew. It was almost comfortable to go back there. So that's what I did. I was pretty much in the hospital from 16 to 19.

Before this happened, I also was dabbling in drugs and drinking and stuff like that, so it all kind of came together. I became very addicted to drugs and alcohol. So I was using that as an outlet. I just hated myself so much. The more weight I lost, I hated myself more. When I gained weight, I hated myself more. I just hated myself so, so much. I was sad, I was mad, I was lonely, I felt... just every emotion you can feel. 'Why me?' That was a huge one for me: I felt really sorry for myself, which didn't help. I felt... really broken, really angry. I felt really alone. I wouldn't let people in.

None of the friends I had in school stuck around because I was not nice to be around. I was always in my own head and I didn't tell people what was going on with me. I lied constantly. I lied to the doctors, I lied to the nurses... even friends that I had on the Unit. I lied to everyone because I didn't want anyone to know anything. It just got to the point where I was so trapped. And when I was 19—that was the last time I was admitted—I got kicked out because I was using drugs on the Unit. And they didn't know for a really long time and then they found out and I was asked to leave.

It's pretty bad when you get banned from the hospital.

When I was in the hospital, I was gaining weight and my eating disorder was active in my mind but not my body, I guess you could say, but my addictions were going strong. And when I went to drug and alcohol treatment, I wasn't using [drugs], but I was using my eating disorder. And to get help with either one, you need to deal with both. You can't just deal with one, because for me they go hand-in-hand.

Basically it got to the point where I was not able to live at home, I had no friends, I had nobody to talk to, I was just really alone and really desperate. That's when I went to—I don't know if you've heard of it, it's a treatment centre, well, I guess it's a home—it's called Mercy Ministries. It's all over the States and they just opened one in BC. It's for women only. It's for girls who have gone through eating disorders, addictions, self-harm, depression, abuse, anything, you go there. It's changed my life completely. I actually knew a girl from 4F4 in 2008 and she went to the one in Nashville and it completely changed her life. I knew about it, but I wasn't ready at that point. It wasn't until I hit bottom that I thought I might as well apply.

Sue: What was so special about Mercy Ministries?

Sarah: That place, for me, was... full of love. That was the main thing for me. At the hospital in Edmonton, I didn't feel like the nurses or the doctors really loved me. Or cared about me. I felt like I was just another problem for them... another number, I guess. Just another hopeless person. They weren't really giving me much hope. 4F4, yes, they saved me physically, but emotionally, mentally or spiritually—nothing. And it is a full body disorder. I think the physical is just a symptom of the actual problem. When I went to Mercy, I felt so, so loved and I felt safe. I just opened up completely and was able to deal with the deep issues. They loved me until I was able to love myself. And it wasn't until I loved myself that anything changed really.

Sue: What did they do exactly? How did they show you they loved you?

Sarah: It was faith-based, Christian. I've never gone to church before this and that's why it was the last option for me. I don't want to become a nun and go to this cult! That's what I felt. But there, they treat each girl as God would see us. They knew my whole file, they knew everything I'd done, everything I'd gone through, but they didn't see that: they saw me as a beautiful girl that's worth something. And they treated me that way, so I saw that maybe I am worth something.

The whole day, everyone is together, so you have constant, 24-hour support. You cook food together, you eat together, you sit with each other, you play games or do whatever. They have a trainer there, so you work out and learn how to do that in a healthy way. They just taught me so much: how precious each individual body is and that it's a gift to us and we need to cherish it and treat it well.

I was there for six months. It's six months to a year—it depends on each girl's journey. A lot of girls, it takes them a while to open up. For me, I was so ready. Before I went, I was on the waiting list for quite a while, maybe six months or so.

Finally, they called to say I was accepted. But two days before I was supposed to arrive there, they called me and said, "We found a glitch on your file." And what happened is, in my past, I'm not sure if it was Dr. O or another doctor, but they wrote in my file that I had anti-social personality disorder, because I never looked anyone in the eye. And that was because I didn't want to tell the truth. In fact, I never told the truth so I didn't look people in the eye. I'd do so many things, like steal, and I didn't show any remorse, because I didn't feel anything. And so I got that label on me. And they were asking all these weird questions like, "What's my anger look like?" They thought I was going to harm people there, so they told me I couldn't come. Which, at that point, I was like 'Where else am I going to go?' Because I'd gone everywhere. It's either I fight for this or I stay the way I am and die.

I went to Dr. O over and over and over—three weeks of craziness—and got her to write letters and I just did everything I could until they said finally were like, "Okay you can come." I think that was a gift now, that happened, because I got there and I thought, 'I'm on thin ice. They don't actually want me here,' so I did everything they asked and followed every single rule they gave me. I was scared to do anything wrong, I guess. So that helped me.

I graduated there, a year ago on November 1. I'll be 23 in January. So, it's taken me seven years to get here. It was very, very long journey and it didn't need to be that long.

The seven years all feels like one big night, like one huge horrible night. I think feeling trapped was really hard. I felt like there was no way out. I just felt like I was falling so hard and so fast and I couldn't get out. I didn't know where to go or who to turn to or what to do. I'd go somewhere and think, 'This is it, I'm going to get better.' And it wouldn't happen. So there was constant letdown after letdown and it was my own doing... it was just really hard. I never wanted to wake up. Going to sleep was my favourite time because I'm like: 'Maybe I won't wake up.' Waking up was the worst 'cuz you wake up and it's (*sigh*): 'Here we go again.' It's the same thing over and over and over again.

• Dealing with setbacks

It was a big thing for me when I realized it's okay to have setbacks. It's not a failure. It's only a failure if you don't pick yourself back up. A huge, huge thing—which I feel is the good thing about eating disorders—is every single person that has one is very determined, because you have got to be determined to act in eating disorder ways, you just have to. It's a matter of turning the determination to something good.

Gratitude lists are a really good thing. My best friend now—we met at 4F4, she's doing amazing and I'm doing amazing—when we were both in the beginning of it, we used to text each other every single morning one thing we were grateful for, like: I'm grateful for... I don't know... the sun. I'm grateful for my mom. I'm grateful for my bed. I'm grateful for... anything. It can be the smallest thing or the biggest. Even if it's the very worst day of your life and nothing's going right at all, there's always something, one teeny, tiny positive thing that you can grab onto. Hold onto that for dear life. That's what helped me. Starting your day on a positive note, can shift your whole day. Because once you're at the end of the day, and it's been the worst day, it can be hard to find one grateful thing.

Resilience is definitely key. I think people can encourage resilience. Like having a family that won't let you stay down, as opposed to somebody's whose family is not really that encouraging or somebody that is by themselves. Encouragement is huge. People saying, "You can do this" gives the person even the tiniest [hope]. Even if they have one—even one person—saying, "I believe in you," it helps. It will sink in somewhere in their head: 'I'm worth it.' It's just a matter of grasping that. I didn't believe it at first.

I had all these positive affirmations and I'd say them. I'd be like, 'This is crap. This isn't real. I'm just telling myself a lie.' But people told me, "You need to tell yourself this every single day, even though you don't believe it... and eventually you will." And it's true. It really works.

But there are people that are really resistant to that. Those are the people that I worry about. You just don't give up on them. You just keep constantly tell them. There was one girl that I knew in the hospital and she's still there. She's been there for years and years and years. And every single day, I text her and say, "I'm thinking of you. I love you. I believe in you." She doesn't respond for months, but every single day I write it, because I know she reads it or, even if she doesn't, she knows I'm sending her one. It's frustrating, but you just have to believe it.

• Recovery

At first, I thought recovery meant learning to deal with—just cope with my problems and to know that I'm always going to struggle with food. It's just a matter of eating, even if I don't want to. But now, recovery is all about moving forward, always living better today than yesterday and striving to move on. Always doing whatever I can to better myself, to better my mind and my body.

I'm very hopeful. Hope, to me, is huge. Probably hope and love are the two biggest gifts that I've received. I was so hopeless. 'Cuz I was always hearing, "Chronic this and chronic that. You're always going to be sick. Blah blah blah." That sucks. That does not make a person feel good. And it doesn't make you want to try because why try if you are always going to be the same?

So it wasn't until I learned that there IS hope, there IS a future past it, there is so much more to life than that and it IS possible! That helped me so, so much. I want girls to know that there is hope, there is so much more than it [eating disorders]. 'Cuz on that Unit, it's like its own little world. I feel like when you're stuck in that, it seems like that's your world and that's where you're gonna be... and it's not.

I was on X mg of *Effexor*, so that's quite a heavy dose of antidepressants. And I don't remember even being depressed when I was put on antidepressants. Anytime I said, "I'm anxious about this or that," they just upped it and upped it. When I came off of it, I felt a thousand times better. I felt sadness more deeply, but I also felt joy, which I didn't ever feel. So that was huge.

• What have you learned?

I guess what I've learned about my mom, for one—and my whole family— is that they love me so much. Even the fact that I was kicked out of my house, I see as a gift, now. I thought that was my parents hating me, but it was actually them loving me more than anyone. Because I honestly think if they hadn't kicked me out, that I would still be doing the same thing. Being enabled by them. Taking advantage. All those things. It wasn't until they said, "No, we can't have you here" that I realized: 'What I'm doing is wrong and people aren't going to put up with it.'

Even having the illness is a gift to me, because, growing up, I feel like I was very judgemental of people. I was just mean and I was not really compassionate at all towards people. Now that I've gone through what I've gone through, I'm not judgemental at all. I know that if somebody is acting out or they look a certain way, I always think there's always a *Why* behind the *What*. There's always a reason behind the way they're acting or what they're doing. So it's helped me deal with so many people and situations and get through life a lot better. Another really great thing that just happened to me is my past feels like a very, very distant memory, which is the biggest blessing I could ever ask for, because it used to really haunt me. So when I think about things, I think: 'Did that really happen to me?' My mom would be a better one to ask because she was actually present throughout it all and I was not. You have no idea what you're doing. [My parents] were experiencing everything right then and there and I wasn't really. That's hard for me, still to this day.

Sue: Do you struggle with that guilt?

Sarah: I used to, definitely. At *Mercy*, they work in modules and one of modules was forgiveness. And I was on it for quite a while. I remember my counsellor was like, "You need to write down everyone you need to forgive and bring it." And I showed up in her office with my name on it and that was it. And she's like, "*Woah*, this is weird." I could forgive everyone pretty much, but I couldn't forgive myself. So I did a lot of work on that. I feel—I still do—like that sucks but there's nothing really I can do, but just walk it out, keep walking it and try to give them better memories today than yesterday.

Sue: Being well is the best gift you can give them. That's all any parent really wants.

Sarah: Yeah.

Sue: What's life like for you now?

Sarah: It's great. I love it. I love loving life. It's amazing, just waking up and being happy and excited for the day. I just have so much hope. I have dreams again, I have goals, I have my family. Everything is so good. Yeah, I still do have bad days, but it's okay today to have a bad day. Everything is good, I'm just happy. I feel because of the struggles I went through, I'm so much more grateful for life today than I ever would have been if I hadn't struggled. Even the smallest thing makes me so grateful, so it's amazing: my whole perspective and thinking has shifted.

There's a line of song, that I really, really love: "I once was blind but now I see." And that's my life. I used to see everything through a really dark, dark lens. I didn't see things properly. I didn't let anyone in and I took everything as negative. Everything was skewed and I feel like that's been lifted. I just see things. Like, "Holy!! The world is amazing!"

Sue: Is there anything I missed? Anything you would like to add?

Sarah: I don't think so. I didn't really know what you were going to be asking, and I was worried that I would get into a lot of my sneaky behaviours, all these things that I wouldn't want to be in the book, because girls don't need to see that.

PHOTO: EILEEN SPROULE

Glenda (Sarah's mom)

"We were just shell-shocked for a really long time.
 You just do what the doc says."

"It's excruciating to watch."

"I think parents beat themselves up all the time."

Glenda: I think it's really important for parents to know what they are getting into. In our particular case, Sarah's dad and I were just shell-shocked for a really long time. And you tend to take professional opinion as the only way to do something. And I think the more people that know there are other options, the better it would be.

Getting a diagnosis was really quite a long process. We knew something wasn't right and we tried numerous doctors. It took a long time until somebody put a finger on it and then it happened really, really quickly. In my perception, we had no time to really consider. We went from "Yeah, there's a problem. We're going to check what it is" to Bang! "This is it. This where she needs to be. This is what needs to be done." It seemed, at the time, there wasn't a whole lot of time to sit and consider. We didn't know anybody personally that was going through it, so you take what the doctor says and you think, 'OK, I guess we'll do that.' We struggled with that for a long time.

Then things seemed to kind of snowball into other areas and you just cope the best way you can and hope you come out on the other side. You hope there's a light at the end of the tunnel... (*laughs*)... and that it's not a train! What I have noticed with time, now that we're all more comfortable with things surrounding the eating disorder—and some of it is trial and error—but, you know... a better counsellor, just a different outlook, a combination of counselling, because, 4F4, I understand it's just intervention, weight restoration, but whenever Sarah was discharged, it seemed to us, like 'Well, what do we do now?'

'Cuz there is no transition. Being outpatient without support, it's just a revolving door because the whole situation needs to be supported. Because change has to happen. Kids come from a situation and they come back to that situation. If they're not thriving in that situation and the situation doesn't change... well, we know what will happen.

And I would say that to Dr. O—she's great—but those kids can't stay on drugs forever and if they have to stay on drugs forever, they're really not making very good progress in the real world. It took us a very, very long time to find somebody that Sarah would talk to. And part of that—I think Sarah would agree—is the person needs to be ready too.

Recovery is definitely a journey, a tough one, and a lot of hard work, with a lot of bumps in the road. One step forward and three back. Or three forward and two back, however you want to look at it.

It takes a lot of patience for all of us, for Sarah, her dad and I. We all had to be patient with each other and supportive, because it doesn't happen in isolation. It's not just Sarah. It's a whole lot of things. I don't know... sometimes we were just hanging on. (*laughs*)

• **What emotions did you experience?**

All of them. I mean everything, from the depths of despair to elation at a tiny step of success. So much fear, I was so full of fear. You just know too much. You know things that you never wanted to ever know.

Sue: What were the hardest parts for you?

Glenda: I don't even know if I can answer that. It's too hard. (*she reaches for a Kleenex*) Knowing now what I do, I would have done things differently.

Hindsight is always lovely. Oh yeah, "How could I have not known? Why didn't I do this different?" That does get better. It does. Some of it will just come from your daughter, saying, "Hey, it wasn't you." When you're in it, it's extremely hard to believe. I mean you talk to people whose child has cancer and they think 'Did I eat something wrong? Did I use the wrong cleaner?' I think anytime things with your children go less than the perfect little plan that you had in place, you blame yourself. Always. I think parents beat themselves up all the time.

Sue: How do we get past that?

Glenda: Nobody tells you that, even if you go in and speak with the psychiatrist. It took me a long time to figure out that psychiatrists really are not very good counsellors—not to take away from what they do; what they do is extremely important in the intervention, I understand that—but you need somebody to deal with your emotions. That's where parents that have been through it can say, "Hey, go to a counsellor yourself. Get your kid involved with a counsellor that they trust because there's so much support that you need." Otherwise, it can basically tear your life apart.

I know that often families implode when there's a physical illness too, but I think it's worse with a mental illness, because it's hard to talk to other people. You can probably talk to virtually anybody about your child's physical illness, but lots of people just don't get mental illnesses. So you feel really, really alone, on top of everything else. They don't get it. For a lot of people, it's denial: "Well, you know, they could just stop if they wanted to. Just make her stop."

Sue: Or "Do you think she's just manipulating you? I wouldn't be so patient. Maybe you need to be a bit firmer." All these little comments. And I know they're trying to be helpful, but they don't understand that I'm in the middle of this whirlwind of self-doubt and I don't need comments that make me feel any more self-doubt.

Glenda: Or minimizing. "Oh yeah, my daughter flirted with that. And it just went away. It's a phase." And I'm thinking, 'You obviously don't understand what's going on here.'

Sue: I just don't have the energy to convince people that it's serious or even to explain it anymore.

Glenda: And that also leads to isolation because you're exhausted all the time. I know I was. It's hard to put one foot in front of the other and if somebody puts up the least bit of... you know... "Get a grip on yourself," you just think: 'Ok, I'm done with you. Sorry.' And you do, you isolate yourself because it's way too much work.

There was a wonderful counsellor who I got the name of from my GP. She helped me personally. She wasn't involved in 4F4, but she knew what went on there. The thing with counselling, it's got to be someone you get along with and trust. I mean the other person who was recommended for the family didn't work. I was OK with him, Sarah didn't like him, my husband didn't like him, so there was no progress there.

My husband helped because basically he wasn't going to give up, no matter what. That's just his personality. Extremely stubborn. We butt heads a lot. Sometimes I thought, 'Give your head a shake. What planet are you on?!' So, in a way, it caused a lot of anguish, but his resolve... (*laughs*) To him, it was inevitable: "It will get better. We're going to beat it."

Hope is really the wrong word. For myself, I just didn't want to consider the alternative. I mean, in that way, I was like her dad: We're not going there. I don't know where we are going, I don't know how, but we're not going there. We're not going there. You go back to when you first have your child, and you're exhausted and you don't know how you could possibly do another thing in that day, but you do. You just do. It takes a lot of inner strength, couple strength, family strength to have that safety net.

And over time, you start to detach yourself in a healthy way from your kid. You know, you start to give them more control and influence over their own direction. You start to feel a little bit better, even though you're not always thrilled with the decisions that they make. You start to remember that they're a kid and they are going to make mistakes and you have to separate what's just a regular teenaged goofball mistake from the disease. And that's the other thing, it strikes at a time where you're expecting a lot of stuff from your kid anyway. It's really hard to not to be in their business all the time.

When you're past the stage where they're telling you your child is going to die, then you start to say, "OK. I can see she's starting to manage." In our situation, some of it was just control. We gave up a little bit of the control and it seemed to be welcomed. I think the biggest turning point was when we decided to—for lack of a better word—back off a little bit, and let Sarah take responsibility, because she had the information. Her body was at a place where her brain could operate properly; she wasn't starving her brain, that really helped a lot.

Sue: Yes, we're trying to figure that out now. How much space to give our daughter, so she can fail safely, if that makes sense?

Glenda: Oh, 100%. And that's what you want with your children anyway.

Sue: You want them to learn, and in order to learn they need to be allowed to fail... but not slip all the way back. So, that's what we're trying to figure out, daily.

Glenda: Wow, if you're doing it daily, you're pretty good. It could be hour-ly or minute-ly (*laughs*). You have to go from being frightened to death that you're looking at your child's ultimate demise to you can see that there is a chance and that they're working towards to it. But you're right, they have to find their level. You cannot make them eat. You cannot make them think any different. They have to figure it out for themselves and that's really hard as a parent. If there was a pill, we would pay whatever price was involved, but unfortunately it's not like that. You can't do it for them, they've got to do it themselves and it's excruciating to watch. It really is.

And as good as 4F4 is—and I understand the economies of scale, there have to be multiple people there—but, you know, there's a lot of negatives that come with the positives and, personally, that would be something I would caution you to look for. Sometimes they learn things that you really didn't want them to learn. That's really hard. And they're so vulnerable. But I don't know how you do it any different. Even in private treatment it happens because they're never just one-on-one. And they still have to be able to operate in society. They need to go to school, they need to have friends, just like anyone else.

• What have you learned through this experience?

To give Sarah more credit for her determination to survive. The biggest thing was when Sarah decided she didn't want it anymore. That's how it appeared. When Sarah was determined to beat it—she takes after her dad like that—when she made up her mind. I mean she was absolutely so determined! But she had to be the one that decided.

I guess I've learned that I'm pretty resilient. I'm proud of myself. When I thought, 'I can't do this,' but I did. You have to have resilience otherwise....

You have to maintain your own health. I can't imagine doing it if you weren't healthy yourself, or if you were in already a really fragile relationship or difficult family situation. I can't imagine. But you do what you have to do. You don't consider the alternative. My child would have to literally be snatched away from me, and I would still be screaming, hanging on.

• Have there been any gifts in this experience?

In all honesty, for myself, I would say no. I know there's things I should probably think, but right now... I'd like to say, "I found..." I didn't. I guess it's like labour and delivery: you don't remember, you just did it. Lots of times, I can't even remember.

Sue: People have suggested that I exhibit the signs of PTSD.

Glenda: Oh and that wouldn't surprise me at all and I probably have the same. I didn't go anywhere or talk to anybody for a really long time. I just did what I had to do.

Sue: You get paralyzed.

Glenda: What you're doing (*writing this book*), is it therapeutic for you?

Sue: Oh yes. It's like entering a haunted house: each family is taking me by the hand and guiding me through, showing me all the things I fear most and then leading me safely out the back door. It's a huge gift.

Glenda: I can totally relate to what you are saying. I didn't know anybody else with it and you don't really become friends with other parents [at the Unit]. They talked about having parent things, but everybody's in a different place. The only parent thing that I went to—and it wasn't through 4F4—was really a bit of gong show. You have virtually nothing in common and you don't even want to be there, on top of everything else. You're just grabbing onto straws. Fortunately, I went with my husband. He's looking at me and I'm looking at him. We made it through but I thought, 'This isn't for me.' I mean, you hear stories but it wasn't necessarily about eating disorders, it was all over the map and you just think, 'Yeah, it could be worse, or it could be better.' It just wasn't helpful.

• Life now

Cautiously optimistic. I mean, on the whole, I don't spend a lot of time worrying, not any more than a normal parent or a parent in a normal situation. I'm very hopeful. Sarah seems to be doing extremely well. She's diligent in taking care of herself and that's very rewarding to watch. She's planning for the future, which is wonderful.

For Sarah particularly, I think the key to staying well, is to care less about what other people think about her, and more about what's important to her. She needs to be confident in her own abilities, because she knows what she needs to do. She's very smart. She's developing a safety net of people and we try to support her the best way we know how. I mean, she's still young, and they do miss a portion of their life—those years when they could have been doing things—and they never get those years back. So there are things that another child may have done then, that Sarah needs to do now. You know, testing boundaries and things like that. Her path is a little bit different than ours, if it works for her, hey, we're all for it.

• Summarizing it all in one sentence

To hell and back. (*laughs*) I know that's a phrase as opposed to a sentence. In my mind, you've seen the gates of hell—parent hell anyway—and you've come back to life, pretty much. There's regrets, but what life doesn't have them? They're just different from other people's. But there's lots of positives. You take a lot of joy in seeing the growth, a lot of pride. You would have never have, ten years ago, conceived of pride in that way. But you do. You think, 'Hey, this kid has got it together.' What I see with Sarah, she's much more insightful than I probably am now. And it could lead to some pretty cool things. She's wise beyond her years and I think that if she stays true to her own convictions, with guidance from people she trusts, she'll be OK.

RESEARCH SAYS

The need for future research has been identified to measure, among other things, the impact of eating disorders on other family members.

— *The Practice Guideline for the Treatment of Patients with Eating Disorders*, Third Edition, 2006, American Psychiatric Association

Treatment fatigue

About two weeks ago, we had a setback. Hannah injured herself so badly, we had to go to the emergency department at 11:30 PM for stitches. I was completely blindsided by this incident, because we had all thought, naively, that self-harm was behind us.

Two weeks later, it seems that everyone in my family has healed physically and emotionally. Everyone, but me. I seem to be stuck in a place of relentless anxiety and sadness. It's as if something inside me has broken. I'm not sure why this is happening now—almost a year into the voyage—when we've overcome so many hurdles, many bigger, many harder. I wonder why my spirit seems to be flagging when all around the signs are saying: You have come so far! You're almost there!

I wonder if marathon runners often feel like giving up at MILE 23? The thing is: I worry that this may not be MILE 23. What if it's only MILE 5? The possibility of so much more ahead, paralyzes me with exhaustion.

When I feel this small and weak, I wonder where my life went. Where, in fact, I went. I think about the things I was doing a year ago and now they seem gut-wrenchingly impossible, almost as if that was another person, another lifetime. I've lost my confidence in the solidity of life and what seemed achievable then seems utterly inconceivable now. I mourn my loss of confidence, even if it was built on ignorance. I mourn the carefree ease of going out for dinner. I mourn the ability to leave our daughter at home alone. I mourn the carelessness with which I used to live my life.

My world has been violently shaken and I can't seem to find my way back onto solid ground.

I know I am telling myself a story of incapacity, weariness and hopelessness. I know we have the ability to frame our story and choose to see any situation, ANY situation, from multiple perspectives. I want to find a different story. I want to feel hope, but it seems so elusive right now. I'm journalling, I'm swimming, I'm doing yoga, I'm reaching out to friends, I'm crying, but nothing seems to be lifting this mood.

My acupuncturist, Andrea, theorized that I am experiencing treatment fatigue and that it is quite normal, after a year, to be here. She suggested that it's okay to change the rules, to turn the light of my life back on and step out of the darkness. Knowing that I am a straight-A student and respond well to tasks, she set me the following homework: Do something that makes no sense to anyone else, that is for no reason, no purpose, just because you want to do it. Something silly, frivolous, strange, fun. Do something spontaneous that might make others question your sanity.

So, of course, I went home and worried about how to be spontaneous! I didn't have any ideas! I asked my husband, "What should I be doing that doesn't mean anything?? Help me plan this!" My husband smiled, "I don't think that's the point, honey."

Yesterday, I was out in the front yard, shovelling the mountain of snow from one side of the sidewalk to the sunny side, where it always melts more quickly. It was really just a make-work project, a way to tackle my frustration with the relentless winter we've experienced this year, but, after a while, I noticed the hole I was digging looked a bit like a mouth. I stopped, made some snowballs for eyes, plucked some twigs for eyelashes and began sculpting a nose. I was on my knees, working at shaping the nostrils, when my neighbours across the street yelled out a *Hello* and *How are you*? I stood up, wet-kneed, snowy-mitted, and said, "I'm good, thanks." Much to my surprise, I meant it.

I'm sure if someone had done a scan of my brain at that moment, it would have shown a very different flow of blood. I felt lighter and happily engrossed for a moment in something that had no purpose, no meaning,

PHOTO: SUE HUFF

no charts, no weights, no vigilance, no monitoring, no past, no future... it was just me and the snow. I was having fun and that, I realized, has been in very short supply this past year.

It reminded me of a photograph I saw of a giant pillow fight in London this week. Hundreds of people packed Trafaglar Square—feathers were flying everywhere—and, in photo after photo, the people looked thoroughly committed to pummeling the stranger beside them. We all need more fun. We need ways to come together and do things that make absolutely no sense at all, because sometimes life makes no sense at all. Kids know how to play and I have no doubt their resilience is tied to a healthy play response. Somewhere in adolescence, we lose the permission to play and perhaps it's no surprise that mental illness begins to manifest in these years. As adults, we move further and further away from spontaneity and play... and further into depression, addiction, marital breakdown, isolation, workaholism, violence and strife.

The photos from London reminded me of a day, about six months ago, when Hannah was still very underweight and very ill. She refused to eat the last half of her snack and threatened to throw it out the window. My son was watching this unfold and it was all teetering on the edge of getting ugly when I suddenly suggested that she should be beaten with pillows for insubordination. My son enthusiastically agreed and we had a mock pillow fight. It was pretty gentle and restrained; we knew she couldn't withstand the full force of our frustration, but playfully, we all let off some steam and then collapsed in laughter.

I think I need to laugh more.

Emma

Age of onset: 14
Age at interview: 17
Treatment: 7 months inpatient, 1 year follow-up

"Your mind is literally torturing you. Nothing you do is right.
Your mind is just eating you alive."

"All I could think was that can't be me.
I can't be in and out of this hospital for 30 years.
I have to get better."

Emma: I was told when I went into the hospital that if I'd waited another week, I would have died. So, knowing that, and the fact that I didn't realize I was dying, you realize how quick it can be.

Sue: Is it hard to imagine being that sick now?

Emma: Yeah, because I didn't see that. People saw it through their eyes, but through my eyes, I didn't see that. Even when they told me I was a week away from dying, 'cuz my heart wouldn't be able to handle it, I thought, 'Oh, they're just trying to scare me. Whatever. Yeah right.' But now, looking back, they weren't lying. They were just being very honest with me.

Sue: That's scary. It sounds like walking with a blindfold and taking it off just in time to see you are on the edge of cliff.

Emma: Yeah, it's exactly like that.

Now I live with really poor circulation, so my hands and feet are always freezing cold. And I have these things tiny red dots on my toes—I don't know what they are called, but they're super tiny, you can barely see them, you almost need a magnifying glass—and if I touch something, even just tap it, it's excruciatingly painful. So when I'm walking, I have to keep my toes up. It's not always bad, it comes and goes. They said it's permanent damage, I just have to live with that, which sucks. I lost a lot of hair, but that all came back. I don't think my hair is as nice as it used to be. It gets really frizzy and dry, and it used to be a lot fuller and thicker.

• Why did you agree to participate?

I think this book is a good idea because reading stories about people who have the same thing, it's really relatable... you don't feel as alone. You learn a lot things. Also 'cuz if you are in denial, and saying, "I don't have an eating disorder," it's good to read it and then you realize, 'Oh, that is me.' Then maybe you go seek the help.

• How would you describe your journey?

Definitely difficult. It's really up and down. Even when you start to feel like you're getting better, or you finally say, "Oh I'm getting better", or people are saying: "Oh yeah, she's come a long way," you still have your good days and then your bad days. You look back and you realize, from Day One, when you were first getting sick, how bad you were, and then you realize how much better you've gotten... but there is still so much more. Even when you're to the point when you're eating what you need to eat everyday, even when you have your good days, you realize there's going to be those bad days that are lying ahead of you. I always say that it's going to be something that I live with for the rest of my life, which is a sad thing to think about, but that's just something that I've just set in my mind. Not that it's weighing me down or anything, but looking back on what has happened, I'm a totally different person than before I got an eating disorder, so I know it's changed me completely. And in some ways, it changed me in a good way, because there's things that I've learned about myself that I wouldn't have learned.

• How did it start?

When I was in Grade 9, I started kind of getting weird eating habits, where I would eat a normal amount one month and then another month, I wouldn't really eat. It was kind of odd. It wasn't something that was noticeable, like I wasn't losing weight or anything. I went into Grade 10 at a fine weight. And then my mom went away for three weeks to Europe on a trip. That's kind of when it began, because no one was paying attention, because my mom was normally the one who was paying attention. For me, a lot of it started, I think, because of family reasons. When I'm stressed, I don't eat. Some people eat lots when they are stressed, some people don't eat. I started eating less and less and then I began losing a lot of weight and then I just didn't want to eat anything. That's when it got bad. I wasn't eating anything in a day really. I was 15, I guess.

After Christmas, 'cuz I was working out a lot too, I was noticeably just too thin. Not in my eyes, of course, but to my parents. I remember, one night, I was refusing to eat. I never ate what they had for dinner, so they made me a sandwich and I wouldn't eat it. I fell down, nothing happened to me, but my mom got all upset: she said I was so thin I could easily break a bone. They took me to the emergency room that night and I just thought it was absolutely ridiculous. I was there all night, a lady did some sort of interview with me. Basically I just slept on some bed while they talked to my parents, really. I remember leaving, and I told my parents it was ridiculous that they'd taken me there and they were like, "Actually, they said it was a good thing you were there."

A few days later, they'd set up a doctor's appointment. When I went in, he weighed me, interviewed me and then he told my mom that I was at a very low weight and he basically diagnosed me with anorexia. He told me I had a week to prove I could maintain my weight. "Yeah yeah, I'll do that." I came back a week later and I'd dropped "X" pounds. He said, "That's horrible."

So that day he sent me to the Royal Alex Hospital. I stayed in the psych ward for probably two weeks, but I don't think the psych ward was a good place for me. There was no one like me there. I was really uncomfortable. I didn't like being there. All the other kids were like, "Why are you even here?" I didn't like it there. I don't think they knew how to deal with people who are anorexic because they said that I was supposed to have X amount of food in a day, but I'd say, "I didn't want to eat it" and I could easily get away with that. And I was in a hospital! So, I was like, "Why am I even here if I can get away with not eating?" I was there for two weeks. I maintained my weight, which is good—if I'd been at home, I probably would have lost—but I wasn't progressing.

I was on the waiting list for the U of A program and the doctor says, "There's a space that the emergency opened up for you. So, you can go there." So I got sent there, with my own room. I thought I'd be there, max, for a month, not even. I ended up staying there seven months, in hospital, sleeping overnight. I started in February and I got out around summertime. I ended up finishing Grade 10 there. I enrolled in the Stollery Hospital School. I actually got really good marks. I slowly progressed out. During Grade 11, I just went every two weeks to get weighed and then after that, slowly, every three months and now it's every six months.

• What were the hardest parts?

The scariest part really wasn't gaining the weight at first, that wasn't the scariest part. It got scary when I realized the amount of food you have to eat to gain weight back. Oh my gosh!!

They say it [anorexia] is a selfish thing, but you don't realize that it harms so many people. The same with someone who is suicidal, they don't realize. I didn't realize that... because I didn't really care.

My friends were good about not telling people why I was gone, but when a lot of people found out, I lost a lot of friends. People are going to talk. They say, "Oh, you're just doing it for attention." And of course that's going to make it worse, because you're like, "That's not why I'm doing it. I really don't know why." At first, I was hurt, obviously. But then, after a while,

I realized if they're not going to be supportive, I shouldn't really consider them my friends.

It takes a lot to figure out why you even did it in the first place. Even now, I'm still trying [to figure it out]. You're never going to be able to pinpoint exactly what it is. Some people are like, "OK, I'm going to diet" and that's how it starts. But a lot of times, it's not even that. You don't realize you're not eating a normal amount of food. You don't really notice. How the eating disorder happens is different for every person. Whether it was personal issues around body image or family issues. For me, it was a combination of both. It started off as being a family issue and then it became a body image issue and then it was all about body image issues.

One of the hardest things, one of the biggest things I used to struggle with is thinking: "Why did it happen to me?" I always look at my friends and I'm so envious of them being able to so easily do what they want, eat what they want and be okay with it. I used to be so jealous. I used to be so hurt by the fact that I have to be this... always... oh, like I'm so messed up or there's something wrong with me.

I had a really great relationship with my auntie, before it happened, but she never came and visited me [at the hospital]. I don't know why. I still don't know why. We've talked and we're a little bit better than we used to be, but it's never been the same. I still struggle with that. I don't hold grudges, but I have a lot of built up anger, I think, still, towards people who weren't there to support me. I can't really wrap my brain around why they wouldn't be there. I feel like if I'd done that to them, I'd never hear the end of it. Also, I just wouldn't feel good about myself for not being there for that person, especially if they're your family.

The most difficult part about it is my family—the way they treated me differently. Even my parents. Not in a bad way. They were very supportive and stuff, but of course, they don't treat you the same. They don't look at you same after you've done something like that. And that, for me, was the hardest part.

I didn't have a good relationship with my dad or my brother, but they made sure to come [to the hospital], at least a couple of times, to see me.

So at least I knew that they were trying. There were just some people who didn't try. There was some people that told me, "I can't come visit you because it's too hard for me to see you." I was like, "Well, OK, that's honest, at least." Or people coming to visit me in the hospital and not even being able to look at me. That was hard too, but eventually you have to come to realize it's difficult for them too.

• Who helped you?

My mom was really supportive through it all. She was always there. We definitely had bad days. I remember I went three days without talking to her in the hospital. That was difficult for me, because I would talk to her on the phone, every day, at least once, if she didn't come to visit that day.

The one person who stood by me the entire time is my best friend. She's been very supportive through it all. She was the one who was there, visiting almost every day. That's what made me realize she is the one person that means something.

Even the nurses in the hospital—they were really supportive. They used to call me their shining star. I was one of the youngest. Sometimes, I see one of my favourite nurses on the LRT [Light Rail Transit] and we'll still talk and she'll tell me about her fiancé. You build such a good relationships with them too; they're always there. They become like your parents pretty much. It was just like having all these moms.

When I first started on the Unit, I was like, "I'm not talking to anybody, I'm not going to talk," but the nurses kind of bring you out of your shell and then eventually you rely on them for literally everything. I remember one day, I just wasn't feeling good, so one of the nurses sat on my bed with me. We just sat there all day and just talked. They're very supportive and they're really good to everybody. That was a lot of help.

As much as I hated going to the group therapies, I think they helped too. A lot of the time, I wouldn't say anything. I would just sit there and listen to other people talking. One of the ladies there, she was 50-something years old and she'd been doing this for 30 years. She'd been up and down for 30 years! And all I could think was: 'That can't be me. I can't be in and out of this hospital for 30 years. I can't be 50-something years old, with kids that won't even come visit me.' That, to me, was one of the biggest things: 'I can't do this. I have to get out of here. I have to get better. I can't be like that.'

I remember another lady, she was a day patient, but she came every day and every day she would refuse to she eat anything. They would have to force her and she would refuse to have the [nasogastric] tube. It was a mess. You could see her lying on her mat, and you knew she was dying. There was nothing to her. You knew... any day now. Every day, you were scared to see her. There's a lot of scary things.

Even one of the girls I became friends with, she had a seizure, right in front of me. And you're like... (*wide-eyed horror*) Afterward, I was sitting with my roommate and she's like, "Honestly, that happens all the time." I'm like, "Are you kidding me?" And she's like, "No, it happens all the time. When you're in here, you're gonna see that stuff." Scary stuff. It makes you realize that you don't want to go back there.

Even today, if I'm about to do something—skip a meal or eat less—then I'm like: 'No! Think about the hospital!' I don't want to go back.

Now, if I'm having a tough time, or there's something that's pushing me back, if I tell my mom or call my friend. Listening to them, hearing their advice, hearing them telling me, "You've already gone through this, you don't want to go back", just reminding me... I think that is very helpful. Definitely, if I didn't have anybody [to talk to], I would still be in the hospital.

• What gives you hope?

I'm a very motivated, very driven person. I have a lot of dreams and aspirations, like the fact that I'm graduating this year and there's so much I want to experience. I want to travel the world, I want to become an actress, I want to become a teacher. I think that's a lot of what gives me hope, keeps me going: there are so many different things that I want to do and I can't do these things if I have an eating disorder and I can't drag my butt out of bed because I'm too weak and too tired. If you don't have hope, what are you aiming for? I think it's one of the main things that everybody needs. I read this quote the other day about hope on Tumblr. It was kind of like— "Without hope, you don't really have a life to live."

When you're anorexic, or have an eating disorder, or even depression, you're not aiming to kill yourself. That's not what I was thinking. If I was aiming to do that, I would have found a lot quicker way to do it! But you don't have hope. You don't really care either way. You're just neutral. While it's happening, you have literally zero hope. You're just walking along. You don't really care. Even when they told me: "You're a week away from dying," It wasn't like: "OK!! Yeah!! Bring it on!!" I was kind of just like (*flatly*), "Oh well, it's okay." Because either way, it didn't really matter to me at that point. You're just defeated. Like someone's told you, "That's it, you're done. You can't do anything. You just have to lie there."

• The thoughts/feelings

I think a lot of it is anxiety. I remember always, always, always feeling on edge. You have a daughter who has it [anorexia], so you can probably tell her attitude is changed. She's probably very angry or lashes out really quickly. One little tiny comment, even if it is meant in a totally different way, your brain is automatically going to switch it to thinking they're taking a stab at you or trying to hurt you or they're trying to make fun of you and you're immediately angry. You have this wall. You're terrified of every little thing that comes at you, every little obstacle.

I remember if I couldn't work out—if I wasn't allowed to exercise that day—I wouldn't even know what to do with myself. I would feel so stressed, I'd feel like there was something eating me alive inside. It's hard to explain what it felt like. It's not fun.

Sue: Sounds like torture.

Emma: It is. It is. Your mind is literally torturing you. Nothing you do is right. I remember I kept thinking: I have to be perfect. If I had one little thing I didn't like about myself—which at that point, I didn't like anything about myself—but if I noticed one thing that day, my whole day was ruined. That's all I could think for that entire day. Oh, [for example] if my arms looked fatter that day, that's all I could think about that day. I felt everyone was looking at me that day because of that reason.

Literally, your mind is just eating you alive. Nothing you say positively [to yourself] will work. Nothing anyone else says to you. Even if someone stopped you on the street and said, "You are absolutely beautiful, by the way." You would think, 'They're just making fun of me.' And you don't realize that it's YOU, it's yourself, that's taking these things and twisting them around in your mind. It's another person inside you, basically, and you don't really see that.

I always got mad at my mom, "Why are you—?!!" She's like: "I don't understand!! That wasn't Emma. That wasn't you. You changed." We'd get into so many fights. Now I see it better, obviously. I realize she wasn't doing anything to harm me, but my mind was taking it in a totally different way. That's all you think: negative things.

I think sadness was obviously a big part of it too, because you're depressed. You're completely depressed. You feel like you're in this black hole and you're stuck in there and you can't get out. You feel like nobody cares about you. And even if people do, you're like: 'Nobody understands. Nobody knows what it's like.' The worst thing is when someone says, "Why can't you just eat? Why can't you just get better? It's all a state of mind." But it really isn't. You have no control over your mind at that point, because something else does.

• Turning points

I've had a lot of issues with my dad, growing up. He's been one of those fathers who's never really been around for us. I mean, he's been here. It's not like my parents are divorced or anything, but he wasn't a good father. He wasn't supportive. I discovered a lot of it [the eating disorder] was a cry for emotion from my father, in a way.

In Grade 9, my parents went through this separation and the way they handled it was horrible for me and my siblings. I remember telling my dad, when he came to visit me at the hospital, "I don't think I will ever be able to forgive you for the way you've been to me for the first 15 years of my life.

The way you handled the separation. The way you treated me during that. I honestly I don't think I'll ever be able to look at you really as a father." I finally just let it all out.

He went home. A few days later, he came back, sat me down and apologized for what he'd done throughout my life and what he'd done during that few months of their separation. I think for so long I'd just been waiting for an apology, a sincere apology and then I finally got. That for me was, such a... PHEW!... a sigh of relief. I just remember feeling so much better after that. Feeling like I needed to get on and move on. Of course, that wasn't the only issue, that wasn't the only reason I was doing what I was doing, but that apology was a turning point.

And my brother too. When we were younger, we were really close but, as he was growing up, he had so much anger towards my father too. He has his own issues, but he deals with them in a totally different way than I do. I still have a lot of troubles with my brother 'cuz he pretty much treats me awfully. Before I got sick, he would come upstairs and call me a fat pig and when I was sick, he called me an anorexic whore. He was awful. He still comes upstairs and says, "You're such a useless piece of shit" or whatever. It still hurts, obviously, but I've kind of learned now that he does care, but he doesn't know how to show it. He gets angry. He gets super mad. So, if I'm sitting on the couch watching movies with a guy, he gets really mad. He's weirdly protective of me, but he's mean about it. I've learned that, yeah, he does love me. He does care about me. He just has a very sick way of showing it.

Sue: And how is your relationship with your dad now?

Emma: Going through the entire process of being in the hospital, I think he realized just how much more support I need, how much I need a dad. So these past two years, I think he's tried. He's not a star father and I don't think he ever will be—maybe that's just the way he was raised—but he's definitely come a long way. He's surprised me, he's been very supportive. I used to think my mom was the only supportive one, but sometimes, he is more understanding or supportive than she is, which is amazing because my mom usually knows my brain inside and out. "Mom didn't understand that, how come you do? I don't get it." He tries harder now too. He'll say: "How is your day at school?" And he never used to be like that. It's nice to have that.

I always thought my auntie was more supportive towards me than my dad ever was... which she was and he wasn't... but it totally surprised me, because my mom and dad were the only two people who tried their very hardest to understand the disease. Which is what my friend did too. She read books on it. She did everything she could. And that's like my parents. Even to this day, they're still Googling stuff. They're just trying their best to learn it. Dad did a really good job. He would go on his own to meetings with Dr. O to ask her questions or email her. It was kind of nice to know they cared enough.

• Defining recovery

That's a tough question. I think that it's... I don't know how to describe it... I feel like it's... jeez... I don't know, I feel like it's never-ending. You are always recovering. Even now, it's been almost two years, and still there's things about me that are not how a normal person eats. I feel like even if I'm at a point where I don't even think about food—let's say five years from now—and I look and I seem like a normal person, I eat like a normal person... I still think I'm always going to be recovering. There's always going to be things that are different for me. Always going to be things that are in the back of my mind.

You are recovering but you are never fully recovered.

I think it's amazing to be here today and then look back on all the horrible stuff that happened just a couple of years ago. It seems like a long time ago for me now, but it really wasn't that long ago. I mean, in the grand scheme of things, what's two years?

I still have good days and bad days. I still have good moments and bad moments. I have more better days though. I still have weird habits. I still do things that are odd but at least I can see that it's not normal. An example: measuring my cereal. I don't know why I'm stuck on it. Measuring my cereal and measuring my yoghurt. Those are two things, for some reason,

I've been stuck on. It's going to take me a bit longer to get away from it.

I still have days where I definitely don't like the way I look, definitely I'm not happy with myself some days. But at least I can wake up some days and look in the mirror and be like: 'Oh, my hair looks good today.' Or I can look at a picture and think, 'Oh I look good in that picture. I like that.' I can at least do that, whereas I can say I never had a moment in those times [while sick] where I liked anything about myself.

• Key to staying well

To keep going. To keep trying and not give up. It's gonna be hard and it is hard. There are days where I wake up and think, 'I don't want to have to eat today. I don't want to have to do it.' But you just tell yourself: "You don't have a choice in the matter. You're going to do it. This is the way it is now. You are now getting better. You are getting healthy and you don't have a choice in the matter." You just think about all the other people in your life who would be harmed by the fact that you didn't eat.

I'm trying this new thing where I never lie to my mom. She likes it if you're very honest with her. Even if you do the stupidest thing, if you tell her the truth, she's okay with it. So occasionally she'll say to me, "Did you eat enough food today?" And I don't want to have to lie to her, if I didn't. So if I don't want to lie, I'm going to do what I need to do, which is: eat.

It's amazing because I realize how much my mind-set has changed. It used to be a priority to have a lot of friends and to be popular. I always thought I wasn't good enough if I wasn't popular or if I didn't have a boyfriend or whatever. Now I realize it doesn't matter how many friends you have. It doesn't make a difference. Having one friend, even if you only have one friend, at least you have one friend that's close. I have the friends I want to be friends with now, who I could see myself being friends with for a long time. They all know [about my eating disorder] and they understand or they try to understand. All my friends have little things that they come to me for help with. And it's nice because we can help each other. My friends are always saying how they're so jealous of my strength and how strong of a person I am. And I always thought I was such a weak person, that I couldn't handle a lot, so hearing that, I think, 'Oh!! that's kind of nice.'

• Summing it up

Recovery was a very difficult journey where I came to discover myself.

Because even though it's been crap and it sucked and I wish I'd never had to go through it, I really believe in that saying: "Everything happens for a reason." You become the person you are, through the things that happen to you. I wouldn't be the person I am today if that hadn't happened to me.

I still have a lot to discover.

RESEARCH SAYS

Using Functional Magnetic Resonance Imaging (fMRI), researchers are able to capture detailed images of the brain while it experiences different stimuli. Researchers at the University of California School of Medicine have been examining the brain activity of people with anorexia and discovered that, even they show less activity in the insula—the region of the brain that tells us whether food is sweet, salty and/or pleasurable. This may impact how people with anorexia experience food.

The insula is also involved in signaling changes happening in the body. This may explain why anorexics experience distorted body image (seeing themselves as fat, when clearly they aren't) and show a lack of concern about weight loss. Literally, their brain may not be sending the "something's wrong" message.

www.eatingdisorders.ucsd.edu/
research/biocorrelatesIPDFS/kaye2010NeurobiologyofAN.pdf

In the depth of winter, I finally learned that within me there lay an invincible summer.

— ALBERT CAMUS

Sandra (Emma's mom)

"All I wanted to do was stay at home, be a mom,
have these perfect kids and this perfect house
and it's never happened. So it's kind of shocking."

- **Why did you agree to participate?**

Because I think if the book gets published, it would have been something I would have bought. We went and got a lot of books, and there are [books with] doctors telling you what they think you should do, but there's not really any with families members saying how they managed to get through it. It's one of those things you don't expect to happen to you and when it does, you don't know where to start.

- **Overview**

Well, I think it started when Emma was in Grade 9, might of been a bit before, but that's when I noticed it. Emma's a perfectionist; everything always had to be perfect and she's always been the most perfect child. We have three children. Our youngest daughter has a lot of health issues. She has a very rare genetic disorder. We had just found out about the disorder and I took it very hard because generally it kills the kids by the time they're 16 and so I went away for a month with my sister on a trip. And my husband's mom came out to stay and that's when Emma stopped eating.

Our oldest, he was diagnosed with Crohn's disease at the same time, as well, so all three of them have had health issues. I think the biggest problem for Emma was that, on top of all this, my husband and I decided to split. He decided he had enough. He was leaving. He couldn't take it because he pretends that nothing's wrong so he moved out and left me with the three kids. I had complete breakdown one day, a complete breakdown, Emma took all that on her. It was hard, hard for her. He was gone for five months... four months? ...this was before she was in the hospital, when I barely noticed what was happening with her.

Emma, because she's always been perfect, she gets more ignored. She's the best behaved, the easiest-going. I sort of wonder if it wasn't just a 'I'm-here too, pay-attention-to-me' kind of thing. So she's had a lot of attention the last while, but not the kind of attention I think she really wanted.

So that summer, I went to our family doctor and just said to her: "I think Emma is losing too much weight, can you talk to her? See what's going on?" The doctor said, "Oh, she's fine. There's nothing wrong." And I said, "No, I think there is. So can you get me an expert to talk to then instead, a psychologist, a psychiatrist, whatever?" She didn't believe me, thought nothing was wrong.

Emma was having circulation problems in her fingers and toes and her hair was coming out in clumps. And I said to our family doctor, "Isn't this going to carry on, and get worse and worse?" "Oh no, she'll be fine. If she starts eating, it will come back." And I'm looking at her, thinking, 'Are you insane?'

Sue: I've heard this from so many families, that the GP is more of an obstacle, a stumbling block, than a help. Family doctors don't seem to be trained to recognise the signs of eating disorders and they don't seem to understand how serious it is.

Sandra: Yeah. It took us a long time to get help. It took us months and months and months to get someone to pay attention to us. I couldn't get in to see a psychiatrist. Finally, I got on the waiting list at the U of A Eating Disorder Clinic and it was a six-month wait to see anybody.

One Sunday, I don't know what happened, but I just packed her up and took her to the Royal Alex emergency. And they put her in emergency care with their psychiatrist at their clinic, but it's only a short fix, where you can come four times, or something.

We got a doctor—now I forgotten his name, he's a child psychiatrist, he's friends with Dr. O—he agreed to see her. So she started to go see him and he kept saying to her, "You're anorexic" and she was quite stunned because no one had said this to her before. She was denying it completely. He said, "I think you should go into the hospital." And she said, "No, I'm not going in the hospital." And he said, "I tell you what, next week if you come back and if you've lost even an ounce, you have to go into the hospital." She said, "Alright."

So, I said to my husband, the following week, he had to take her; I wasn't going this time. If [the doctor] put her in the hospital, I wasn't ready to drive her. And so he called me and said, "I'm taking her right straight to the hospital." She'd lost another X pounds. So they put her in the psych ward at the Royal Alex Hospital. She was there two weeks, at least. Staying there was quite an eye-opener for Emma. That night, I took her up her things, we got her room all set up.

I think it was two weeks later the doctor said to us, "I've got you in with Dr. O. She said to us you can put her right in, she can live here or she can come here for the day and for meals." I said, "No, I want her right in the hospital. I think that's the best thing." She moved in. She did her Grade 10 at the hospital.

She was down to X lbs, I think. She was pretty scary-looking and some of her room-mates were even scarier. They'd been doing this for so many years. Her first roommate, I think this was her third time at the hospital. She was 21. Beautiful girl. So pretty. You just think, 'What a shame.'

Sue: How did you get through all that?

Sandra: I don't know that I have! Some days, I'm okay. Some days, I still have my moments. I got myself a dog... 'cuz my husband hates dogs, so he moved out and I bought the dog. The kids were quite happy.

I've always been that kind of person that I think nothing bad is going to happen to me. So maybe I feel like this it's a just sort of bad dream and I'm going to wake up. I guess I've always wanted just to have a peaceful home, which I haven't had. I'm always striving for that.

I don't know why I've made it through. Maybe I'm stronger than I think I am. Life isn't always perfect, or what you think it will be, but you make it through.

• Hardest part of the journey

I guess it's the frustration, not being able to do anything, or not being able to get through to Emma. I try to talk to her. I try to make her understand high school is a drop in the bucket. This is really a minor part of your life. You've got so much to look forward to. I find it frustrating. And so scary. You never know what they're going to do. I still find it scary. I still wake up every day and think, 'Please let her at least eat something different, not measure/weigh her food.' She thinks I get mad. I'm not mad, I'm just scared. I'm just worried for her. I'd hate to see her relapse.

I find it to be a heart-breaking, lonely journey.

So, it's hard to talk to people about it because they don't understand. I'm a very easy-going person. I'm too laid back maybe. People might think, 'Oh, you're not strict enough with her or you should force her to eat.' They just don't get it.

That's where I find it to be lonely, because there's no one to talk to. And my husband is not much better. He's of the idea: she's a girl, so I should take care of the situation. I really don't feel like I have anyone I can talk to about it. For me, the last few years have been a lot of frustration, being scared, sad, depressed, guilty. Very guilty. I kept thinking: 'I could've done this. I wish I could've gone back, I would've done this different or that different.' Guilt was one of the biggest things and I think it still is.

Sue: How do you process that guilt? Because guilt can be so corrosive.

Sandra: It is. Yeah. I'm probably not the best person to say what I do with it, because I don't think I'm good with it. I know quite often I'll say, "I should never have been allowed to have children. I've done such a poor job of raising my children. I've caused them so much unhappiness." You think you're doing the right thing. I guess nobody knows what the right thing is.

Sue: Hindsight is painful. And we have to learn to forgive ourselves and believe that we made the best decisions we could at the time. We can't go back. We can only go forward.

Sandra: Yeah, that's true. Unfortunately.

Sue: Do you think there's a difference in the guilt felt by a parent if the child has a mental illness or a physical illness? Which type of illness provokes more guilt?

Sandra: I think I feel more guilt about the mental illness. I guess because I feel that—it might not even be true—that I have contributed more to the mental than the physical, because of how she's been brought up, or the circumstances she's been put under that she wasn't capable of handling, which, I guess, is ridiculous because a different person would've handled it just fine. So, obviously, it was something in her brain from the start.

You just want them to be happy.

I've always been a stay-at-home mom; I haven't gone to work in 20 years. I'm here all the time, every day with them. I think that's how come I noticed that Emma wasn't eating, quicker than maybe other parents might have: it wasn't that she had lost so much weight; I just noticed the change in how she ate and her personality, because I do spend so much time with them. In my whole life growing up, all I wanted to do was stay at home, be a mom, and have these perfect kids, and this perfect house... and it's never happened. So it's kind of shocking.

I think part of my kids' problems is that I don't like them to be sad or hurt or upset. I'm always trying to make sure their life is running smoothly. They've never had to deal with unhappiness, I've tried to cover it up, which hasn't been a good thing.

• Defining recovery

I sort of feel Emma's still is in the recovering process. She still hasn't recovered, to me. Recovery to me would be that she's happy with herself.

And she can eat a piece of cake, if she wants to. Or if she's not feeling well, OK, she doesn't have to exercise that day. When I can see she's happy with herself, and more relaxed—because she's not a relaxed girl—then that, to me, would be recovery.

Sue: Some people have told me recovery is a process. It's not like taking a cake out of the oven: "DING! You're done!"

Sandra: And that's what I had hoped! I thought she'd come home from the hospital and she would be "Emma" again, that she'd be all better. So that was sort of a shock.

We have a condo in Florida and when she got out of the hospital in June, we planned a trip. I said she could bring her best friend—they've been best friends since Grade 5—and the three of us went to Florida. I had really high expectations of this trip. My sister and my mom kept saying, "I don't think you should take her. She's not well enough to go yet." I looked at them like they don't know what the heck they were talking about. "No, I'm taking her; she'll be fine." And she wasn't. It wasn't a good trip at all.

People often think that anorexic girls — I shouldn't say girls because boys get it too — anorexic people can seem very self-centered. It's a very self-centered disease. Living with Emma, I see why they think that. On this trip, she was just so mean and cranky and demanding. And her best friend was just stunned, didn't know what to do with herself. I think she wanted to go home the second day she got there.

At first I tried humouring her and then I got mad at her. Then my husband arrived with our other daughter. His family from Quebec arrived as well. He was getting worked up because, of course, they wanted to go out for meals but she wouldn't eat when we went out. One time she ordered a vegetarian burger and it arrived and it had some little bit of sauce on it. No way! Because she didn't know what that sauce was and how many calories it was. She had a big scene at the table. And when I say big scene, I mean everybody was turning to stare at us. It was just a nightmare. Crying. A nightmare. It was too soon. My husband... he's not a good kid person. I knew that before. If he's in a crisis, he's even worse.

Sue: How does he feel about you doing this interview?

Sandra: He didn't seem to have a problem with it. He probably would've chatted with you too if he'd been here. You know, I shouldn't say he hasn't changed, because he has gotten better. I think he tries a little harder to show Emma that he loves her. I know he loves her, but he's not good at showing her and she needs that. He's still not the best, but he's gotten a bit better. I think the whole thing was very scary for him.

Sue: Who supported you through this?

Sandra: *(long pause)* I'm trying to think... *(long pause)* I don't know.

Sue: Some parents have turned to counsellors, for themselves... did you do that?

Sandra: No, we didn't. I have some good friends that were pretty good. Some were not. Some were ignorant, didn't want to see Emma, wouldn't talk to Emma, were scared to go see her. Some were really good. I guess my husband was a good support—we chatted, the two of us—which was probably good. We depended on each other. And my mom, much as she was not very understanding, she was very supportive, in that we'd go pick up Emma together and take her out for coffee or take her to the library. My mom would go with me all the time to the hospital. She did spend time with me and with Emma. So, she was good. She was probably the best one. Sometimes it's nice to have someone go with you up there [4F4], because I found it to be quite a depressing place: all these girls lying on mats on the floor. That was shocking to me too: how many girls there were there.

We decorated Emma's room quite a bit, brought up her own bedding, did a whole wall of family pictures, inspirational messages on her wall. We tried to cheer her room up quite a bit. It's gloomy up there. It seemed so dark to me all the time. I don't know why. It always seemed dark. It would be nice if it had a huge, big room with some sofas and chairs and things. The TV room is not very big.

• Turning points

It all sort of flowed along slowly; there hasn't been really any big turning points. She continued to go up and see the psychologist and the dietician and get weighed. And then she decided she didn't want to see the psychologist anymore. She didn't like him. I don't know why; he seemed like a really nice person to me. I liked him. But she didn't want to go anymore. When she left the hospital, we were kind of forgotten about. I thought they would follow her more closely, that Dr. O would still see her now and again. I found that hard.

Sue: When they come home, it's suddenly all in your court, as the parent. That transition can be hard. I remember once, I was preparing a scrambled egg for Hannah. I put a little bit of oil in the pan, so it wouldn't stick. And she refused to eat it. I was so fed up. I said, "Aren't you bored of this?! Because I am. I'm so bored of this! It's just a little bit of oil. It doesn't make any difference. Eat the egg!!" She wouldn't. Absolutely refused. I had to throw it out and do another egg, without oil. A few days later though, we were referring to it as Egg-Gate. You have to laugh. In the moment though, I just lost it.

Sandra: That's nice to hear, that others do [lose it]. Because I always feel so guilty, if I get like that, Emma says to me, "You get so mad at me." It's 'cuz you're so scared and you're caught up in that moment. It could be, like you say, an egg or something else minor, but you're looking at that egg as ALL FOOD. It's scary.

I know Emma still has a lot of problems with her feet and her fingers. She has these little sores from lack of circulation and she'll complain about them every now and again and I know it's wrong and I shouldn't do it... I say to her, "That's what happens when you starve yourself to death." I know it's probably not the right response, but I just want to be sure that's she's well-aware that this is the consequence of not eating correctly and if you do it again, you're going suffer even more. It's probably not the thing to say, but I do it every single time. Or she'll say, "My hair isn't as thick as it used to be."... "That's what happens when you starve yourself." I do it constantly. Constantly.

Emma's at that age where she's pushing the boundaries and I worry. Our oldest is a boy, he's 20, I didn't worry as much what he was up to as I do her, which she finds unfair, and yeah, I'm sure it is unfair. I don't know what the difference is truthfully—having one girl, one boy, doing the same things—I don't know why I feel more stressed, overly protective about the girl, but I do. I guess I worry more about Emma. She's a little sensitive. So I could say something completely innocent and she's jumped that into a huge, big story about how I don't love her or don't care about her. I find her more difficult nowadays than I used to, before she got sick.

Sue: Sometimes I find it hard to know if a behaviour is just normal teenage stuff or if it's related to the eating disorder.

Sandra: Yeah, you're right. You're never sure. Should I be a little more sensitive about this or should I just be strict about it?

• What gave you hope?

I think, Emma did. Because she's a very smart, very personable kid. I see a lot for her ahead. Just watching her, how hard she worked, her struggle, how much she worked towards getting better, that gave me that little lift. "OK, if she can do this—this is harder for her, than it is for me—if she can do it, I can do it." I just thought: I have to be there for her, so I have to get my act together and be there when she needs me, not be this blubbering, whiny mess that's going to fall apart. (*laughs*)

I'm really proud of far she's gotten and I probably don't tell her that enough, because I want her to get a lot further. I don't want her to live her life like this. To me, it's still heartbreaking.

A study at University of California School of Medicine explored the altered dopamine function in people who have recovered from anorexia. In the study, subjects were given amphetamines. People who did not have anorexia displayed a normal response to the amphetamines: they experienced a sense of euphoria, brought on by the release of dopamine in the brain. However, recovered anorexics had an unusal response to dopamine: they experienced elevated levels of anxiety.

For most people, eating tasty food produces a release of dopamine and pleasure, signaling the brain, "Yum! This is good!". If, as the study suggests, dopamine release in the brain is anxiety-provoking for recovered anorexics, this could contribute to the high levels of anxiety they experience while eating.

By contrast, starvation and strenuous exercise activate the reward pathway in people with eating disorders (Bergh & Solderstein, 1996; Casper, 1998) flooding the body with endorphins which are chemically identical to addictive opiates (Huebner, 1993; Marrazzi & Luby, 1986).

"Starving, bingeing and exercising all serve as drug delivery devices as they increase the circulating levels of endorphins." Because endorphins affect the brain exactly the same way opiates do (like morphine or heroin), these endorphins are potentially addictive.

web4health.info/en/med/docs/p010259.html

Jenn

Treatment: Outpatient
Inpatient (multiple times)
4 months at Ottawa Hospital

"I often forget I'm 25. I feel I'm still 19, because I had four years that I wasn't living. It was like it was stolen [from me]."

"Three years ago, I couldn't walk. I had trouble breathing. Recovery is learning to be alive again."

• Where does your story start?

Jenn: I've always felt really embarrassed about it, to be honest, because it happened to me a lot later in life. It didn't get sick until I was 19 or 20, in my second year of university. It was my first time away from home, my roommate was putting me through absolute hell. No family, no friends. I got a stomach virus and I couldn't eat anything. [Food] just kept going through me, going through me and I went to the doctor and they were testing me for Crohn's and everything else. Nothing was working, and I'm thinking, 'Well, I can't keep going to school and on the bus for two hours a day if I'm constantly running to the washroom,' so I just started eating less, because then you don't do anything. And once your appetite starts decreasing, it's just not there anymore.

One day, I went shopping and I tried on some pants—the size I would normally wear—and it was like hey, these are kind of loose. So I tried on a smaller pair and 'Wow, I've never worn this size before'... and it kept snow-balling and going and going. It wasn't really about the physical or getting compliments; it became kind of a game almost: "OK, I had *Fruit-To-Go* yesterday, I only had half of one today. I only had carrots for lunch..." It kept going and going.

My mom kept saying, "Jenn, I think you have an eating disorder" and I said, "No, I think you're crazy. No. I don't starve myself; I eat all the time. I don't throw up." The tension between us was growing. My boyfriend and I were at each other's throats 'cuz I was grumpy all the time and I was always angry. Every little thing would set me off. And then I was getting scared to go out to eat and I was getting obsessed with food because I wasn't eating.

I had gone to see the doctor with my mom and he even said, "No, she doesn't have an eating disorder, she has a stomach thing, and we need to get her to see a specialist, but just to put you at ease, I'll give you a refer-ral to the U of A, to Dr. O." And I thought, OK, just to satiate her, fine. I didn't really want to go, but I went to talk to Dr O. We chatted about the cards [for healthy eating] but I wasn't admitted. I was diagnosed with IBS and we were to keep an eye on colitis.

I was having trouble preparing my own meals and I was thinking that maybe I might start the [eating disorder] program as an outpatient, so I went in to get weighed and I looked at Dr. O and I said, "I think I'm going to faint." I just fainted right away. She called upstairs and they took me in right away, and hooked me up to an IV. I called my dad 'cuz we were supposed to be going out for lunch that day and said, "Hey Dad, I don't think I can go out for lunch today" and he goes, "Oh why?" And I said, "Well, I fainted and I'm in the hospital" and I just remember him saying, "Jenn, Jenn, Jenn." He said, "OK. Don't phone your mom, I will call her. I'm coming right there now."

I went in that weekend and was getting an ECG and Dr. O looked at me, point blank—she's very to the point—and said, "Ok you're going to have a heart attack and die if you don't get some potassium." I said, "Oh, OK.

I guess I'm not going anywhere." My boyfriend and I broke up that weekend. I had lost all drive for anything.

I started the outpatient program. That was a very interesting process. I was doing really well. I was taking summer classes at the U of A. Everything was going really well. I was a full-time student in September and kept getting my lunches and suppers at the U and I had a new boyfriend... everything was good, good, good. I was at my goal weight, I got discharged.

And then next... when was it? I started relapsing again in the winter. And then I went back and Dr. O said, "You should probably come back now." So I did that again in the summer and that really wasn't much fun because the rules were a lot stricter now that it was the second time. I was still doing outpatient. I got totally better.

So, I decided to go back to Ottawa. I was doing well for the first bit, then: major relapse. It kept snowballing. And then I came home for Christmas and my parents were not pleased with me whatsoever. They were so upset. Each time it happened, I was significantly lower [weight] than the previous time. My parents were like, "You should go back into the hospital" but I wanted to finish my semester.

So I went back [to Ottawa] and I was doing so-so. I came home again for Reading Week and it wasn't very good, so I spent a week in hospital in February, revamping, and then I went back and finished the semester and then my mom came to see me and I wasn't doing good at all and she flew home with me. I was there again for the summer. Dr. O said I should be an inpatient. We had a big, big fight about it. My dad didn't want me to stay there. I went through the summer and I got (*making air quotes with her hands*) "healthy" again, went back to Ottawa for my fourth year.

I came home at Christmas and honest to God, no one in my family would even speak to me. Except for my one sister-in-law and she's like, "Jenn, I know that I don't have exactly the best track record but I'm not going to treat you like you don't exist because that's ridiculous. I'm not going to keep you from seeing your niece." At that time, I didn't have any relationship with my nephews because they are developing and my family didn't want me around them with weird eating habits, because kids pick up on things really fast. And it was the worst, worst, worst three weeks of my life. And my grandpa was really sick at the time too. I promised him that I would get better.

I went back to Ottawa and for the first week I was there, I was really fuzzy. I was slurring my speech. I couldn't walk. I couldn't bend my legs. I didn't know what is going on. And I just thought, 'OK, I'm just tired because I took the Red Eye [overnight flight]. It takes a little while to get back into the swing of things.' But later, my roommates took me to the hospital. I was taken by the nurses to an examining room and left there for ten hours, by myself. And I'm freezing. The doctor comes in the morning and says, "Well, your sugars are really low. I just think you need some glucose." Sent me home. Nothing. Whatever. He didn't pick up on the anorexia at all. I used to wear three pairs of pants to school in the winter, I was so thin.

Watching me at that time, was like one of those mimed shows on the Comedy Network. Getting out of my car, I'd have to open the door, lift one leg out because I couldn't bend my legs. Then I'd have to turn slowly, lift the other leg out. Grab the top, pull myself up, close the door as best I could. Walk around, straight-legged, try and grab get my backpack, put it on, then walk up the step, one step at the time, one foot at a time, get my keys ready—because I couldn't open the door at the same time and pull it—so I'd open it with the key, stick my foot in there somehow and wedge myself in and then pull it open. And, thank God, we lived on the ground floor because I was right there. But then my bedroom was in the basement, so anytime I needed to go to the bathroom in the middle of the night, it would take about 20 minutes.

I refused to come home at Reading Week that year. I would Skype with my parents and turn off the camera and tell them the camera wasn't working. But my mom came to visit in March because she just had a feeling. She had a dream I was shrinking and shrinking and shrinking then all of a sudden I was just gone. She woke up crying and decided she would come visit. I got checked out at the doctor, my reflexes weren't working. Apparently, when you go through the process of flying, with the change in altitude, your reflexes can actually stop working, if you don't have enough internal power. They don't need to work as opposed to your heart or your liver, so they don't work anymore.

• Getting admitted to Ottawa Hospital

My mom was...[so upset]. Even to that day, I was saying: "I need to go to school, you can drive me there, but I need to finish. It's my last semester. I need to graduate." We were waiting for a bed in Ontario and even looking at the States. All of a sudden, the Ottawa Hospital called: I got a bed. I did not want to go. I yelled and screamed. I don't think I've ever been that mean to people. I was livid. I was yelling.

I had to do that horrible phone call to my brothers before I went in to the hospital in Ottawa saying, "I don't know if I'm going to make it." Having to make that phone call, it was shocking. Because at my sickest, it's hard to believe now...um... I weighed X pounds. My niece almost weighed more than I did, and she was two and a half years old. I had no muscular structure at all. I don't even know how I was living.

The program at Ottawa Hospital is only six people and you are all in-patients. They expanded the beds to seven for me. I started in the program and it was completely different. I was there from March to June. I came home. I kept in touch with my dietician. Even when I was living in Australia, she would call me every week. For the past three years, I've had no relapses. I haven't looked back.

Sue: What is it different between the two programs?

Meal programs very different: at U of A, it's a calories program and before that I had never counted calories, after that, I became obsessed. The Ottawa program is completely on exchanges, like the diabetic: a grain is a grain. One piece of advice: Don't start counting calories, because that will screw you over. The calorie counting becomes extremely obsessive. It's better if you never start that.

Nobody sleeps in hallways in Ottawa. They are not heavy on medication. "If you feel you want it, we will talk about it." They only weigh you once a week, so you aren't getting super-stressed because you are getting weighed every single day, because you shouldn't be. Your weight fluctuates. It's more normal to do it on a weekly basis.

Every Tuesday morning, Dr. B would meet with the inpatients. You have a journal, you are required to write in it. He would specifically ask you how you think your week went and you have to talk in front of everyone in the room. There are no private meetings. Any questions you have for him or the nurses, you have to ask in front of everyone. So if you say, "I was constipated yesterday," you have to say it in front of everyone. And for me, that was really difficult. You have to share everything. But that's how he tells if you are getting better: what you are going through. And any one of the patients can comment on you. It's very intimidating. It's extremely group-intensive. You are there all day, every day and you are in groups. You have a schedule. If you are five minutes late, you are in trouble. You move as a group. We did everything together. So you get to know those people really well.

Every Wednesday, we would have to order a dessert from the cafeteria downstairs—like a cake or something—and you have to challenge yourself. Every week, you would make a weekly goal: a food goal and a physical goal, so it wasn't just about food. Like someone could say, "You always wear such and such clothes on Tuesday when you get weighed. Next week, you should try wearing something else." And you'd have to do it, because the group holds you accountable. Or someone else might say, "You should go a whole week without wearing makeup, just to see what it's like."

And then we would have one day a week, we would order [food] as a group, instead of just our individual trays. But we were never allowed to use measuring cups, so we'd have to know what a scoop of potatoes was like and the dietician would watch us to make sure we were doing it correctly. Another thing, we all had to eat at the same time, so you couldn't start ahead without everyone starting. You could finish ahead of others, but you couldn't leave the table until everyone was finished. It was awesome. We had a really good group. It was like having dinner with friends. We'd have the radio on and play games. If you could see someone really struggling, you would start up a conversation to get their mind off it.

Once a week, we'd go out for snack together. And once a week, you had to order from the cafeteria, like a hamburger or whatever. And you have to challenge yourself, you couldn't order the same thing or the other patients would get mad at you. It was the most annoying thing ever—but probably the best thing—how the group held you accountable. People didn't believe I couldn't eat dairy; they thought it was just another way of restricting. So, I had to eat a yogurt, have a really bad episode to prove that I couldn't eat it. That was annoying.

The biggest difference between the U of A and Ottawa is the *Ensure*—if you miss one pea at the U of A, you'd have to *Ensure* it. *Ensure, Ensure, Ensure.* All the time. It was so unrealistic. That's not what happens in the real world: if the toast is burnt, you don't *Ensure* it. And the levels! I was up to two trays of food, I'm only 5'3", I can't handle all that food and I'm not supposed to. That never happened in Ottawa.

Friday, Saturday, Sunday, there was no program, so you could get a pass for the weekend. If you did really bad on the weekend, the doctor wouldn't take your freedoms away. He would right out ask you why you did that and you would have to talk about it. If you asked for a pass for the next weekend, he would say, "OK, go try again."

At the U of A, the nurses interact with the patients [in a way] they feel they are very above [you]. They treat it as their job. In Ottawa, the nurses were scary as hell when you first got in there, so you knew they were in charge, but after that they were so much fun. If you want to go for a walk, they'd say, "OK, go ahead but you will need to make up for it when you come back." So you would add an extra apple or whatever. Because they trusted you, it wasn't so maniacal. And you weren't trying to outsmart everyone, so you ended up being more honest about it.

Also in Ottawa, they have a policy that if you are below a certain BMI, you had to be in a wheelchair, no ifs, ands or buts. You weren't allowed to walk. It's harder to get around in a wheelchair. At the U of A, I was on an IV pole; I walked everywhere.

• Who was instrumental in your recovery?

My mom and dad. I've put them through a lot and I feel terrible. It almost tore a wedge between them on how to deal with it. It's such a selfish disease. I closed myself off and just kept thinking, 'You guys don't care about me. You're not doing anything.' Now I can see all things my family did for me, all the time they gave up. It really strikes me: they love me that much. They've been there for me, through everything.

My dad is a man of few words. He's not an emotional guy, but he would sit with me every night when I was staying at home and he would read a meditation to me every night. "Close your eyes, get into your space." And he did Laughter Yoga with me: one person has to go, "Ha!" and then the other person goes, "Ha! Ha!" and then you would be laughing. And it felt so good. It was amazing. Before I got sick, I never really had a relationship with my dad where I had a conversation about anything other than hockey. We really have a good relationship now; we talk a lot.

My grandma and grandpa have always been very supportive and concerned. I wanted to get better for them. My grandma doesn't judge. I can talk to her about anything. She's been a huge help. My nieces and nephews: I wanted to be there for them. My brother and I got a lot closer. And my friends have never left my side. My two cousins, that I'm closest with, they've been there forever as well. So I've been really lucky 'cuz I know people [with eating disorders] lose a lot of people in their life. I do have some friends who found it extremely difficult to watch me go through that and they closed themselves off, because they couldn't deal with it. I've had to come to terms with that. That's OK. That's how they dealt with it and they couldn't do it any other way. I have to respect that. It hurts. It sucks.

My [high school] friends in my home town, we don't talk about it. We go out and have fun. They might talk about it, behind my back. That's okay. In Australia, I had a relapse, but I got through it entirely on my own. I didn't go into treatment. I didn't let my family cook my meals. I was 23, 24. I took care of myself. I was building relationships, I was making friends, I joined a campaign, I had all these new experiences. I started yoga. I had the best year of my life last year.

Yoga made a huge difference. Being mindful is very important. It really helped. I was living around the corner from a studio and I was practicing every day. It wasn't about the physical [exercise] after a month. I felt so good. I was eating well. I was having a social life, and you can't do that without going out for food. I got around my head. All of a sudden, it wasn't there. I was free. It was so weird. When I went back to Ottawa, I was so worried I would get triggered, but I didn't. It was like seeing it for the first time, because all the time I was there [before], I was sick. I didn't get to know the city or do anything.

I often forget I'm 25, I feel I'm still 19, because I had four years that I wasn't living. It was like it was stolen. I didn't have the university experience I should have had. I was focused on being sick. That takes all your energy.

• How would you describe recovery?

Basically, recovery is learning to be alive again. You have to learn everything again: Learn how to eat again. How to live again. It's indescribable. Unless you go through it, it's very hard to understand.

It's been really hard for my grandma because, when I was sick, she had always said, "Oh, I just want my Jenn back." I would feel terrible, because I couldn't give her that. It's not possible. I can't go back. That's not me. I'm not 10 years old. I won't ever look like I did in high school. You aren't ever going to have that person again.

Recovery is a process of having to prove to everybody—but also to prove to myself—that I'm who I am, I'm comfortable within myself, so I don't have to regress to who I was before. This is me. And you have to accept that. Because I've always been very concerned about what everybody is thinking and if everybody is okay. I've always put myself way last, always made sure everyone else is comfortable before I am. Now I've gotten to the point, where if you don't like it, that's your problem, there's nothing I can do about it. I've done what I can.

Sue: Can you describe your emotional journey?

It's definitely been a roller coaster. Up and down. Angry, fearful. Scared that I will die. Panic attacks. Feeling terrible that I can't give enough, can't produce what people want, I can't be perfect. Not good enough. Very angry: Why did this happen? Why can't I get rid of it? Why can't I lose enough? Gain enough? Why, why, why?

I felt very sad that I've missed out on so much. Very sad that I haven't been able to be there, because I've been in the hospital when my nephew is having a birthday party. That I've lost relationships. But it's also been really joyful in the fact that I've had to get to know myself. I got to know who I am, what I want out of life and how to get there. I've met amazing people and learned so much from them... and there's no thanks enough to give for that. I've built new relationships with people in my life, like my mom and dad. We're on a new footing now.

I've gone through craziness, absolutely hating every part of my mind and wanting to throw it all away, to loving it, coming to appreciate it and what it can do.

• What is the gift of this experience?

I've learned that everyone is vulnerable. I never thought this would happen to me. I mean, I thought girls who get eating disorders are 16 in high school and worried about how they look. No, that's not how it is. This can happen to anyone.

I've learned you can recover. It is possible to get better and be well again and have a life again. Because when you are in the middle of that pit of despair, it's never-ending. I've learned to see the world a lot differently. I've gained self acceptance that I probably didn't have before.... that was just masked by confidence. You actually see how important your relationships are because, literally, you are on the brink of losing them or you are on the brink of dying. People who have been on their deathbed will tell you that you learn what matters and what you need to work on. And what's the most important.

There are still times when I get nervous if we are going out for dinner. Every day, it gets less and less. Each time I do it, it gets easier.

Since this interview, Jenn has become a certified yoga instructor, has moved to the UK and is engaged to be married.

RESEARCH SAYS

During starvation, both grey and white matter of the brain shrink. These changes may also trigger or accelerate behaviours and symptoms associated with eating disorders. In particular, scientists have been focusing on a part of the brain called the anterior cingulate cortex (ACC).

A study done at the University of Iowa (Carver College of Medicine) showed a 15% decrease in the volume of the anterior cingulate (ACC). Other studies have continued to investigate this particular region of the brain which appears to be more affected than others by starvation.

http://ajp.psychiatryonline.org/article.aspx?articleid=99289

Decreased volume in the ACC has also been noted in patients with obsessive or compulsive behaviour.

http://www.ncbi.nlm.nih.gov/pubmed/20923432

When the patient's body weight is restored, the brain volume returns to normal in the ACC. This brain restoration is linked to preventing long-term damage and multiple relapses.

http://www.ncbi.nlm.nih.gov/pmc/articles/PMC3652574/

PHOTO: SUE HUFF

What breast cancer taught me about anorexia Part 1

On April 16, 2013, almost exactly a year since Hannah's diagnosis, I wrote a single word entry in my diary:

Lump?

The next day, I went into the doctor, had a mammogram and ultrasound, which she said "didn't look good". I was booked for a biopsy the following week and what I somehow already knew was quickly confirmed: I had breast cancer.

It was hard to accept, after the struggles (and triumphs) of the previous 12 months, that our family would once again have to face the uncertainty and turmoil of a serious illness. As one of my friends said, "I file that under UNFAIR." As we all struggled to find our footing, I kept a close eye on our daughter: How was she coping? Would my news trigger a relapse? She had come so far in a year and was rebuilding her life, her health, her friendships, I hoped that she wouldn't be knocked off course. But a month after my diagnosis, we were hit with more hard news: she was relapsing. We discussed options for treatment with her doctor and she was adamant that she wanted to be admitted as an inpatient.

"I want to stop this. I don't want this to be the rest of my life and I don't want to become that person again who is nasty and pushes everyone away. I've made friends with a really special group of girls and I don't want to wreck that," she said.

I was impressed by her maturity, her clarity, her determination but felt unsure: inpatient? Wasn't that a bit drastic? Surely, it wasn't that bad. Her weight was nowhere near as low as it had been last year. Couldn't we tackle this at home or an as outpatient? As we did it last time? She said, "I know you can, Mom. I've seen you. No one doubts that. I just don't want you to. Not this time."

My husband was clear: with my cancer diagnosis and all that the treatments would take out of me, he didn't think we could handle both at the same time. He was proud that Hannah was taking ownership of her illness. He sensed that she needed to discover her own strength and independence, as well. We were told there were no beds available for at least a week, so I held out hope that a successful week of refeeding at home would convince our daughter to reconsider. But one day later, unexpectedly, a bed became available and we were asked if we wanted it. I wrestled with the decision and wished we had more time.

I asked my husband, "Do you think I'm just putting it off? Do you think she'll be exactly the same—or worse—in a week's time?"

He simply replied, "Yeah, I think so."

Through tears, I said, "I don't know how to make this decision."

"Maybe we should ask Hannah what she wants to do," he suggested.

Earlier that day, I had told her: "Whatever you decide you need to do to get better, I will support you 100%." I didn't expect to have to walk the talk so soon. I couldn't hide my grief and I didn't want my tears to influence her decision. So my husband talked to her alone, while I cried in the back yard. When he posed the question, she thought carefully and decided: yes, she wanted the bed.

Thirty-six hours later, she went into the hospital, with her suitcase full of clothes, her threadbare stuffed unicorn, Una, and a very ratty quilt from her childhood that I spent two hours hastily patching up the night before. There is a particular pain that you feel as a parent leaving your child in the hospital. It is too hard to describe, so I won't even try.

For the entire previous year, I had fought against her being admitted as an inpatient. I felt somehow if she stayed close to me, I could keep her from being swallowed whole by this illness. But now, I was faced with complete surrender of my child. I thought of Jack's courage driving back and forth to see his daughter from Rocky Mountain House. I drew strength from his determination.

For twelve months, I felt like I had waged a war against a relapse and now my greatest fear had come true. I remembered the parents who had bravely soldiered through multiple relapses and I was comforted by recalling the interviews with their bright, successful, joy-filled, "in recovery" daughters. If Hannah can be like them after this, it will be worth it. Still, I cried at the sight of her empty bedroom and felt the gaping hole in our home, as we set the table for three instead of four.

And then, cancer marched in and forced me to let go. It was simply impossible to hold both ropes at the same time. I think Hannah knew this all along; I just needed some time to catch up to her innate wisdom.

As Hannah and I both moved through our journeys to health, it was hard not to see all the parallels:

- We both had to face the uncertainty of our illnesses and the frightening possibility that it might re-occur at another point in our lives.

- We both had to come to terms with changes to our bodies that affected our sense of self, self-confidence and security.

- We both had to endure treatments that made us feel worse in order to be healthy.

- At a biological level, both our illnesses were bound to estrogen.

- And as much as our journeys involved physical realities, the steepest hill we had to climb were internal, psychological and emotional. We both battled anxiety, "what ifs" and the seductive undertow of negativity.

- In order to heal, we had to let go of each other, be separate and draw on our inner resources.

The separation was a bigger challenge for me, I think. Through Hannah's illness, I felt a need to protect, to supervise, to monitor, to evaluate and plan and anticipate. At points, it felt that her very life depended on my vigilance and foresight. It was exhausting. Many people tried to counsel me to disentangle myself or to let someone else take the job of Watcher. But, as the parent of a minor, as her mother, I felt responsible for her and, ultimately, somehow, I felt responsible for her recovery.

My acupuncturist wisely reminded me, again and again, "This is her journey. Not yours." But I couldn't truly accept that. What happened to her mattered so much to me, it seemed impossible to separate. My whole life had been turned upside down by her illness, my every waking moment was centered around her illness, my schedule, my hopes, my fears: everything seemed tied to her recovery. My life had become her journey. It felt too risky to let go and just watch it unfold. Everything depended on it.

But something significant shifted inside me when I had to share the news of my cancer diagnosis with Hannah. Distraught, she exclaimed, "Why do these bad things keep happening to me?" And I said, "Honey, this isn't happening to you. It's happening to me. Of course, you are affected and it's okay to be scared or sad or angry, but I need to be really clear: this is happening to me, not you." As I heard the words leave my mouth, I thought, "OH! And that is of course 100% true for her illness too! It's happening to her, not me!" The penny finally, finally dropped. I realized too a harder truth: it wasn't just her recovery I carried, I also felt responsible for her illness. "This wouldn't have happened, perhaps, if I had only...."

I tried over and over again to root out that weed of guilt and blame, but it was always there, beneath the surface. At times, I had felt twisted by the burden and the pain of guilt would spark reactions in me that were disproportionate or inflamed. People would ask me, innocently or ignorantly, what caused her eating disorder. Everyone wants to know causes, I suppose, so they can feel safe and separate, but I heard accusation in every inquiry and would immediately feel the need to defend against the folkloric theories of the "controlling mother" or the "demanding, A-Type, perfectionist mother" or the "negligent mother." Mothers get a bad rap when it comes to mental illnesses in their children. Once people have decided on the cause, it's easy to look at any mother and see evidence to support your theory. At least, that's what I felt people were doing when they looked at me.

Ironically, the spectre of blame also arose with my cancer diagnosis, under the label of "stress" and "a stressful year." I realized that some people might think that the stress of Hannah's illness had caused the breast cancer to manifest, but I have a family history of breast cancer (and other cancers) that, literally, requires two pages to document. Truly, the odds were always against me. If stress had any part to play in "turning the cancer on", that was a final ingredient in a long and complicated stew that was put on the stove a long time ago. In the same way, Hannah's illness was lurking and got turned on by a series of unfortunate coincidences. No one is to blame. Sometimes, shit happens. It's bad luck mostly. Seeing this from the vantage point of my own illness, helped me to let go of the idea that I caused her illness or could have done anything to prevent it from happening.

ORIGINAL ART: PARRY WYMINGA SCOTT, AGE 13

Message to others with eating disorders

"As someone who has experienced it first-hand,
what would like to say to others who are struggling
with an eating disorder?"

Jenn

The first thing you need to understand: You didn't make yourself sick. It happens. It's okay. It's a disease and food is your medicine. You didn't choose to be here and you don't just "choose" to get out it. It's like if someone is diabetic, you can't say "Hey pancreas, you need to make more insulin." It's an illness.

The next step is you doing something to get out and you can do that. It might not be telling yourself: "I'm going to get better." It's using the supports that are around you and going through the process and just allowing it to actually work for you.

Everybody is different. Everybody's treatment is different, everybody's coping mechanisms and everybody's transition to getting better will be different. So what that looks like for you is not what it looked like for me. There is no actual concrete "something" I can tell you to say: "Hey! This is how to get better." But you will find a way to get through it. And you can find a way to get through it.

Sarah

I think even though every girl's story is completely different, the feeling is the exact same. So, I'm hoping that the girls that read the book aren't just saying: "I'm not like that, I didn't do that," but they see: "I feel like that."

Julia

I know, I definitely know, what a person who is underweight is going through, in terms of dreaming at night, and all you can feel is your tongue getting fatter in your mouth, and you are like, "What the heck is this?" Or your skin stretching, or your legs aching because they are suddenly getting nourished. I can totally empathize with that. The phantom feelings you have during the day. In the long run, being at a healthy weight, and also a healthy mind-set is ten times better than that. I don't remember much from that time period; my brain was nothing.

So, I guess the hope part of it... is that there is something better in life. There's so much more that you can be. Don't let that thing control you. And there is that light at the end of the tunnel, although it may look very small, right now.

Sarah

[When people are sick] they really aren't there. Your thinking is inwards. You're always thinking about yourself—not in a selfish way—that's how it works. It's really hard to reach them. I don't know. Maybe just hug them all, and say, "You're worth it, please, believe me." It's so sad. Nobody, not even the worst human, deserves to suffer like that. It's horrible. It's absolutely horrible.

Hailey

I feel like nothing you can say to them can make a difference when they are in that mind-set. I don't know what advice to give, honestly. Just keep going. Because it's going to be shitty and it takes a long time, but it gets easier and easier and easier. And good days start happening more and more often if you keep trying.

I've been trying to recover for five years. I've come a huge, huge, huge, long way. It's very, very helpful to have a goal. I've seen a huge difference in this last two years. If you asked me before if I could have anything in this entire world, one wish, what would I want? It was: "To Be Dead." 100%. But now, it's "Happiness" and I've pretty much got it.

Emma

I know for me, at first, I was in complete denial. I mean, probably ever body is at first. You don't want to admit to something like that, but once you do, I think it's important to open yourself up to trying everything that the doctor is telling you to try. If you're in the program at the U of A, make sure you go to those group therapies, even if you think that they're pointless. Even if you go and you don't want to talk, it's so relieving to sit there and listen to other people talk too. It helps you a ridiculous amount.

I focused a lot when I was there—which I don't think anybody else should do—I focused a lot on making friends [with the other patients]. I think too much. I ended up making this one friend and she was really suicidal and it was just a bad, icky friendship for us, because I totally neglected my own treatment to help her. I spent an entire month just caring about her, only.

You need to get rid of those friends that aren't being supportive too. When I first lost my friends, I was "Oh my gosh." But then I realized afterwards a lot those girls were just bringing me down even more, making me feel insecure. Because you need to surround yourself with a great group of friends.

For me now, I have this group of friends and we're really supportive of one another. None of them is perfect in every single way. Every one has their own different flaws, but they're all completely beautiful. It's nice to have a group of friends who I can go to whenever I need and say, "I'm having trouble with this and this." They just sit there and listen and sometimes they give you advice.

That's one thing every girl needs: even one person they can talk to and open up to. 'Cuz you can't keep it in. You can't hold it in. 'Cuz you'll never get better if you don't let it all out. If you're holding it all back, then it's just denial and you're not going to be able to feel better. Because I didn't talk about it. Even when I came out of the hospital, I wouldn't have done something like this [interview]. People would say: "Hey, where were you?" I'd say, "Oh... you know. I was just kind of sick. I didn't eat very much." I didn't tell anyone how serious it was. But once you're willing to admit what happened to you and share your story, I think you realize it's helping you and you're getting better.

Jenn

To the younger girls dealing with bullying, I would say: there is so much more to your life. When you get older, you can go and do whatever you want... there's so much out there. You can hop on a plane and be somewhere else. There's your whole life ahead and this is such a small part of it.

Lauren

I would say: "You are beautiful".

Emma

I think a lot of girls go on the internet, they go on Facebook, they go on Tumblr and if you are really struggling, like I was, the best thing to do is to turn that stuff off for a little while. I think [the internet] makes it harder on you. You go on Tumblr and you see all these pictures of these girls and all you can think is "Oh my gosh. They are so perfect. I want to be just like them." But it's not what a normal person looks like. I remember that was a lot of what I struggled with: looking at magazines and stuff. For other girls, my advice is don't look at that stuff.

Olivia

I think the biggest piece of advice is you have to want to get better. Because it's a part of yourself that you have to get rid of and that's hard. It's really hard to let go. Harder than, I think, a lot of parents and even a lot of doctors realize. It is literally a part of you that you are giving up. That loss is really hard. You feel like you don't know what to do with yourself. So, you need to remind girls that you build yourself back up. Yeah, you might be letting go of something but you're going to get so much back from it. So you have to want it in order to get better, 'cuz no one's going to make you better, you have to make yourself better.

Jenn

People ask if you're ever really get cured... there's always little things or there will always be that time when you feel bad about yourself or think "I don't want to do this today", but that's normal. Don't second guess yourself and think "Oh my god I'm relapsing". It's totally normal. Once you accept that, you can move on with your day.

Lauren

I would say: "Don't place your worth in things that are constantly changing." I placed my worth in men giving me attention. If I wouldn't get hounded one day, I would be like "Oh you must have gained weight, you're not good enough." I would get so hung up on it. If you place your worth in things that are so ambiguous and changing, you are never going to feel good about yourself, ever. That was huge for me. Everything was about moving targets. I never got the satisfaction that I'm good enough where I am. Who you are in this moment is good enough.

My counsellor tells me, "You can't have a job where there are moving targets." I used to be a waitress and my boss pushed 'til I was going to break. I would take five tables and I'd do a really good job, so he'd give me more tables and more tables and eventually he had it so I was the only one working the whole restaurant. Because I could do it. He would push me, push me; he never said "This is good. Do a good job where you are at." It was toxic for me. Your worth can't be in moving targets, things that change, things that other people set for you, it's really dangerous. And then you just break down.

Sarah

I know this isn't possible, but one thing I always wish that I could do is take a little bit of my hope and package it up and give it to them. Just so they can have the slightest feeling of hope, because that's huge. If I could sit down with them one at a time, I would just to tell my story 'cuz I feel like if they can hear the story and hear from somebody who's been exactly where they are... just to show them that it's possible to recover.

Sue

To me, you are all living examples of hope—the fact that you survived and that you're willing to share your story. You give me so much hope and I hope others can feel that too, when they read this book.

PHOTO: EILEEN SPROULE

Message to parents

"What would you like to tell other parents
who have a child with an eating disorder?"

Rena

Keep going, don't give up. Realize that it's a marathon, it's not a short distance run, you're in for the long haul. So you need to make sure you pace yourself that you just don't put all your eggs in one basket, and then when there's a relapse, your whole life is destroyed. So celebrate the small successes and realize that you are in for the long haul. Keep looking forward. Keep looking ahead.

Kim

I remember Dr. O saying this to me, she said, "It will take at least a year. Don't be looking for this to be fixed quickly because you're with us here now at the hospital. You need to think at least a year." So just take a breath and realize it is going to take time and it's little itty bitty steps. For every three [steps] you go forward, there's sometimes four you go back, but that's okay. You can't allow their disease to take you down too, because they need to have someone there—who's in their corner—which you are, of course, because you are driving them to their appointments and everything. You see it that way, but they just see it like Mom is dragging me there again. They're not going: "Mom sure is nice for picking me up and rearranging her day." So you can't look for those things in your child's eyes to be successes because they aren't going to see it that way. You just need to slow down and not try to rush things. Everyone gets there, but there's not an exact time.

Sue

Having no idea how long this will take or how it will unfold is very disorienting. I feel like I'm swimming and I don't know which way is up.

Rena

I would say look lot longer time. You are looking in weeks and months. But where are you going to be in two years? Where are you going to be three years? Have a longer perspective on it. Your daughter will be much healthier (in two or three years), she's going to be more mature. She's got the support now, she knows where she should be and with the supports, she'll get there.

Sue

This illness can really rip holes in your confidence in your abilities as a parent. It's made me doubt myself. And because my whole focus right now is to help her recover, a setback for her feels like a failure on my part.

Rena

Your priority is obviously your daughter, so maybe that's where you get your sense of accomplishment and peace: I am successful in monitoring her. Are you doing a good job? Yeah, yeah, you are, because that's your priority. But you are walking along side her, not doing it for her. You are doing a good job of walking alongside her. So if she takes a step back, you are still there with her. That's when you reach back and pull her alongside.

Sandra

You have to have a lot of patience. A lot of patience! I think you have to pay a lot attention to your kids. You have to be really careful and watch what they're doing. You have to be very, very diligent in watching what they're doing. Which I am. Like I say, I'm not strict, and I get criticized for that quite a bit, but I do pay attention to what they're doing. They think I don't, but I do. Patience is, I think, my biggest thing.

Lots of love. Because without patience, my gosh! I'm a very patient person. I'm very easy going. I can go for a long time before I blow up, but even I found that it was a lot.

Helen

Educate yourselves as to whatever the latest research is out there. Educate yourself, don't give up and to give your child unconditional love and support. Definitely.

Sue

What would you say to parents of children who are over the age of 18 and the child is refusing treatment?

Helen

Talk, talk, talk. Keep those lines of communication open with them. That was the one question I asked Julia's doctor, when she had phoned me one day at school. I said, "What can we do to help her? She is not getting it, and she is so stubborn, she always has been." Her doctor said, "We could get her committed." But that's through that legal process. I was not willing to take away her self-esteem. I was not willing to do that to Julia, to say, "I am taking all rights away from you." I would not do that to her. (*sigh*) So, I think it's basically about keeping those lines of communication open. Unconditional love and support.

Sue

With any challenge I've faced, I jump in with both feet. If it's hard, I just try harder. But with this illness, that doesn't work. It's forcing me to shift, almost on a cellular level, how I do things.

Ryan

Don't try to fix it. Don't try to fix it. That was me. By the nature of my gender, I feel like when something's broken, I have to fix it. I saw it with my mom, my dad, my sister. With my sister, a couple of times. Once I drove in December, all the way to Vancouver to pick her up and bring her home and to finally put this thing to bed, to finally save my sister. Another time, she's suicidal around Christmas time and I get the call, "I'm going to kill myself, I need help." "I'll be right there." I drive, pick her up, drive to the Mis [Misericordia Hospital], sit in the Mis for eight hours. Finally, we get in, ten minutes before the doctor comes in, she says, "You know what? Watch this..." The doctor comes in, "How can I help you?" and she says, "I'm perfectly fine."

"I guess you can go home."

I'm like, Are you kidding me?! There came a point, where I went, ya know, as much as I want to—and I still want to—I can't do it for my sister. It's all up to her.

Kim
But I think as parents. I don't think that's true. I think you can do something as parents.

Ryan
Do what?

Kim
I don't think you wash your hands and say, "I can't do anything."

Ryan
I never ever once said you wash your hands. I think Olivia has 100% control over her health. You have none. You have the support mechanisms, but the reason why Olivia is doing better, no offence to you, has nothing to do with you. It has to do with her, with her acceptance, with her ability to look herself in the mirror and say, "I will take a *Prozac*. I will eat my sandwich, I will report to my doctor that I was puking." End of the day, my opinion, we can support her, but ultimately what happens with her is all up to her. She's the one who's going to say, "I'm worth it. I deserve help."

Sue
I think as parents, we so desperately want our kids to see themselves as we

see them: beautiful, full of potential, worthy, loveable. Can you give some-one else a sense of self-worth or is it something that comes from within?

Kim

And there's a whole shift, in child psychology, about parents who are rais-ing their kids with charts and stars for everything. So, it's "Yeah! You got up and came to the table! Let's give you a star! And when you get 20 stars, you'll get this or that." And the kids get too wrapped up in their self worth being about... a star. Instead of saying "Great job! You got an 80! " or "Oh you got an A+!!" You know what you need to do, on those things that aren't perfect is say: "I can see you are trying really hard and that's what's important. And you need to do the best you can do, and if the best you can do is a 60, then that was your best, and I know you worked as hard as you could." But not to be always acknowledging and rewarding for every little thing because then we raise kids who are out there, looking for little things all the time to make them feel better. And they need to know that their worth is not wrapped up in those things.

Sue

So, we send the message: Your worth is not your mark on a test, your worth is not your weight, your worth is something much deeper than that.

Kim

Yes, I think so.

• About self care

Glenda

It's so important to do some things for yourself, to try and keep a sense of perspective. It seems like you start to just fall down the rabbit hole and it consumes your whole life and it's so unhealthy. And it's not helpful to the child because they start losing perspective as well. It seems that they need to see that you're strong, and that life is going to go on and that they're going to turn it around. And that's a hard balance. Cuz you don't feel it.

Sue

My husband and I started taking a Latin dance class. Sometimes, we are just too stressed to remember any of the steps, but we still go, every Friday.

Glenda

I applaud you for doing that. I think that is really critical, in my mind, for you and your husband, but in retrospect that's something that the child can look at and say, "Hey, the whole world is not going to hell in a hand-basket because of this." 'Cuz that's got to be really scary for them. There is a sense of normalcy. Also, the child needs to know that in that very short space of time, that they need to take responsibility for themselves. Because there's no reason they can't reach out, in this day and age, with cellphones and texts and all of that, if it's something that is totally unmanageable, they could reach out. But for that little window of time, it's them and they have to say, "Hey, in this hour, I'm going to be responsible for myself." So little by little... you hope.

Val

One of the things Hailey is learning in DBT is to celebrate the small things. And you too, you should do that. I mean go get your feet done, when it's 40 below, on a day, where—you know what—things are OK today, so we're not going to think of the past or we're not going to think about Friday. Today is Wednesday. She's good, I'm good, I'm going to do something nice for myself.

• Impact on the whole family

Sue

It's hard on the other sibling. They don't want to add to the worry, the burden. And my son keeps insisting: I'm not the one who's sick. I don't need any help.

Glenda

I've so heard that. That is something else I think that people don't really think of, it's the family situation. I hesitate to call it a family disease, but for lack of a better word... Whatever is going on, unless you're a family that never interacts, it affects everything. It affects what groceries are in the house, it affects how much time you have for the other child, it affects whether he's going to bring friends home. Every little nuance of your life is impacted, nobody is protected or left out. It can be really good... I won't say good... it will be an important learning situation for him. Males typically don't like to get help.

You are in crisis mode; anybody who is faced with a desperate situation with one child, that's where your focus goes, and that would be in any type of situation. The other child is just existing and they're young adults and their needs to be met as well.

Jack
We are so focused on the one child, that we forget to take the time with the other child. Go for a walk or go for a drive with them.

Glenda
I certainly would encourage you and the members of your family to really explore ways to be stronger, because it affects everybody. The family has to function, so the sooner you can get doing it, probably the better. Sarah has an older brother and his journey was not that pleasant. The siblings are worried to death and they're mad and they're all over the map. Cuz they're kids too.

Sue
It feels like I'm walking a tightrope everyday. I have a day when I think, 'Okay, I got through that bit alright' and then you turn around and realize, 'Oh, I dropped that.'

Glenda
Yeah, that goes on for a while and you have to forgive yourself. Nobody knows really how to do it. Sarah has to forgive us, when we screw up, because we're only human. Do the best you can. That's all you can do.

Jack
I think a lot of parents they blame themselves for it, they take all the guilt

for themselves. It's harsh but you punish yourself for your child getting sick. "What if...??" It's brutal. You need to come to terms with it doesn't matter what I did or said, it's what I have to do now. I'm going forward. That's hard, though.

Val

Parents need to remember: it's not about you. It's not about you. It's not about you. It's not about you. It's nothing you did. It's nothing you said. It's not that... it is so environmental, and biochemical, and societal, if anything we could do, is to change the magazines and the *Victoria's Secret* models. Ironically, her friend who is still on the Unit—she's a severe, severe, severe bulimic—Hailey learned so much from her about how out of control your life can become at the very, very, very lowest point. Remember when she was going to hotels and meeting with guys...remember that?

Hailey

And sleeping with them for binge money. She was a Catholic girl, she's a virgin, never had a boyfriend, never kissed a guy and that's how bad it got: she had to get binge money for her food and the only way to do it was to sleep with guys. So she made a *Plenty of Fish* [dating website] account and that's what she did.

Val

She went to Kelowna with that one guy for the weekend and used you for an excuse. Really dangerous stuff. The manipulation, the lies, the lows that they can go on, the things that they'll do. Like go to a drug dealer's house looking for cocaine. The things they'll do. That this devil, this eating disorder, makes them do. It is unbelievable.

Hailey

It's a different person.

Val

It takes away who they are. So if I were to say something to parents: What you're seeing in the throes of this disease is not your kid, it's not your kid, it's not your kid. It's not your kid.

Hailey

It's this disease.

Val

It's the demon that's living inside of them right now and it is curable...
not even curable, it's...

Hailey

It's treatable, I'd say...

Val

It's treatable. You can learn to live with this, where "Ed"—that's who we call him in our house—doesn't own you anymore. Guilt is a waste. You have to do nice things for yourself. You have to be good to yourself. And you have remember that your child is a completely separate entity from you. Your kids shouldn't be a reflection of you, they shouldn't be, a reflection of your success or failure.

This eating disorder is a very selfish thing. It makes everyone in the house selfish. The person who has the eating disorder is selfish—unbeknownst to them at the time—and it's almost contagious, where everyone in the house becomes bitter and selfish. You just want some peace. You want to go to bed and not have this thing with you.

Sue

I need to maintain a sense of optimism for my daughter, so she can see that hope in me, but also not to deny what I'm feeling. It's hard to find that balancing point.

Rena

So then I guess my question to you, is do you have someone who can walk beside you and encourage you and say, "Yeah, remember you're supposed to be doing this. Or: It's not about you." You have to be able to acknowledge what you're feeling, express it, or journal it.

Sue

I have this incredible friend whose daughter is going through exactly the same thing. We text each other every day. I don't know what I would do if I didn't have her to walk this path with me.

Jack

You guys are each other's rock. You are reassuring each other. You are supporting each other. You can say whatever. I think one of the other things too [that helped me], is a counsellor I've seen, for myself. She said to me, "Your life is like a tornado that's spinning out of control right now. You can't fix everything." She said, "What you need to do is grab one thing from this tornado. Reach it, grab it, hold it and fix that problem."

I think through everything, that's so true. You need to let go and focus on what you need to focus on, what you need to get you through that day. It is very overwhelming. You leave your bills sitting there. You can only do one thing.

Glenda

Parents need to know that there is hope. It's ugly, but you will get through it. I understand there is a small percentage that don't.... Don't give in, don't give up, love your kid and do the best you can.

Jack

As hard as it's going to be, every morning when you get up, plant both feet on the ground, hold your head high and proud, and know who you are and believe in your children. Keep putting one foot in front of the other.

Sue

Thank you. Only parents who've been through it, can truly understand this journey.

Jack

You will get there. That's the biggest thing is not to give up.

Geneticists at the Children's Hospital of Philadelphia are looking at genes that pass on the risk of anorexia. Also, Cynthia Bulik at Faculty 1000 Medicine is exploring the brain protein BDNF, which has been linked to self-image, anxiety and depression. BDNF levels are low in anorexics but return to normal with weight restoration, so it may be a useful biomarker to track recovery.

www.eurekalert.org/pub_releases/2009-06/fo1b-maw062309.php

What we wish people understood

"What do you wish people understood about eating disorders?"

- ### It's a serious illness, not a choice

Jenn

People think you just want to look like a supermodel so that's why you are sick. They don't understand it's an impulse and an addiction, because once you start doing it, you're actually addicted. Once you get those endorphins into your body, you have to keep doing it. With the anorexia, you get on a power-high when you're not eating all day. It's a serious illness.

Cassie

People think girls are doing it to just to get attention and a lot of people don't take it seriously. That used to bug me because a lot of people don't have enough information. They say stupid things. They don't know the actual effects. I'd just like people to know it can be deadly.

Jack

I'd want everyone to understand that you can't just make that person eat. And that it doesn't matter what you do, it's the individual themselves, it's their mind, it's a sickness. It's not a choice. So many people don't understand that.

Hailey

Just how serious it is. Everyone thinks it's just a little phase that these girls go through, but it's not at all. It's really serious. It's not you trying to go against your parents. It's not you trying to rebel and not eat because your parents won't give you a car. It's like a voice inside your head constantly telling you these things. You have the realistic side of your mind and you're like, "OK, I'm going to eat," but at the same time, you just can't. It's the weirdest thing. So the thing I want people to know is that it's a mental disease, for sure. It's not learned. It's really frustrating how everyone is like, "OK, snap out of it now." It's hard. Do you think I like living like this?

Sandra

That is the frustrating part for me too... how judgemental people are about how you're handling the situation. You just want to say, "OK, you come and deal with my family for a few days and then you tell me what I'm doing so wrong." With our youngest daughter's [genetic] disorder, she has limited hearing, limited vision, it attacks her heart, her kidneys, her liver and it makes these kids really large, really large. Well, people judge us all the time, that we've fattened her up. That isn't the case at all. She's like this from the time she was two. We'd go out somewhere and people would comment—comments we'd get about bringing this "big, fat child into *McDonald's*." It was unbelievable how judgemental people are. She's hard to deal with, she doesn't get things the same as a normal child. You can't reason with her. People just don't get that. Nope. Nobody. No one. And it's the same with an eating disorder: you can't reason with them and people just don't get that. "Tell them they're going to die and they'll start eating." No. I tried that. I tried everything.

Olivia

That you can't just stop it. You can't "Just eat." It's not that easy.

Sarah

I used to have people, all the time: "Just eat something, just go eat steak." I would be like, "That's actually really..." I would cry. First of all, that's really hurtful. I can't.

Glenda

Well I guess, it's just would be part of the whole continuum of disease and mental health and how interwoven they are. 'Cuz there isn't "Well" and "Not Well", it's a continuum. And it shouldn't be shameful. It shouldn't be any different than juvenile diabetes, you know. It's just something that has occurred and needs to be dealt with and we can all learn something from it. People are scared. They're afraid to ask you, because they're going to upset you or they don't understand or they assume things.

Emma

You look at cancer, that's obviously something that person didn't choose to have, that's something that happened to them. For me, I think having an eating disorder is the same. You don't choose to have it. Nobody understands that. A lot of people say it's a mind thing.

"You could easily turn it off, you can turn it on." Whereas somebody with cancer has to go through the treatment. Well, so does someone with an eating disorder. Once you have it, it's not something you can change. You have to go through treatment just like a person with cancer has to.

Even when my mom, when it first happened, that's how she thought too. She'd be like: "Why don't you just sit down and eat?" When it was brand new to her and brand new to everybody else. Even me, I didn't realize. I would say, "Yeah why can't I sit down and eat?" Well, I can't. I literally can't do it. I can't. I can't do it. Nobody fully understood that. A lot of my friends too were like: "I don't understand it." Even people who said they did, they didn't. They were just saying that to be friendly. To keep me quiet. Not a lot of people fully understand.

Rena

Some people would just kind of downplay it, not realize how serious it was. Even a friend of mine at nursing school, I shared with her about Lauren's struggle and she said, "Oh yeah, I went through that, don't worry about it." Other people had been, maybe, having bulimic tendencies but they never got hooked. I thought, "No, no, no, no, you don't understand. It's way worse, it's not just a phase she's going through, it's way worse." People didn't know how serious it was.

Julia

From my own experience, being pushed: "Eat, eat, eat... you gotta eat to get better." But hell, I'm not going to gain all the weight today. It has to be a slow, steady process. In general, I'd like people to understand the recovery process. Pushing food on me will make me want to push it away. Letting me take my time, take the steps when I'm ready. And just knowing what's going on in my mind. It's a constant battle of Yes, No, Yes, No. Yes, we're going to walk home; No, we should take the bus. It's that constant battle. For the public just to be aware what's going on in the mind of someone with an eating disorder and how to approach that.

Lauren

I think that they find it very simple: girls want to be skinny so they have an eating disorder. Maybe that's how it starts, but it's so much deeper than that. For me, the eating disorder wasn't a result of wanting to be skinny, but it was from a core belief that I was an inconvenience, I wasn't good enough, I was a failure. [The food] is not the only part that's unhealthy. It's the core beliefs about themselves. If you get them to stop puking or you get them to start eating, they aren't better. You have to go so much deeper.

My counsellor, he is really interesting. I've seen psychologists, psychiatrists, everything about this and they are always trying to give me tips on how to curb my symptoms—give me meds to calm me down, whatever. But he says, "I don't care. Everyone deals with stress in different ways and if you binge, that's fine. I just want to get to the root of the cause of it. Because you know what? That works. That's a good stress reliever," he says that to me. "It works. But that's not what I want to talk about." He doesn't talk about my eating disorder, he doesn't talk about my failures. He doesn't talk about any of that. We talk about all the deeper stuff. It was really profound to me: he doesn't ask me if I've binged or purged today. I've come a long way since seeing him. It's so much more than what you think it is.

And also that it is an addiction. Absolutely addiction. I don't think most people realize that. I think about what I did to keep my addiction alive. I'm an honest person, but I would lie to my parents. It made me someone who is so much different than I am. It is just such an addiction and you need to treat it like one.

Rena

It's the duplicity, I think. That's their struggle. It makes it probably even more difficult to acknowledge their eating disorder because then they're going to be disappointing everyone else. People say: "I want my daughter to be just like you" and then they're feeling phony. "You don't really know me. If you really knew me, you wouldn't want to have anything to do with me." It sets them up for even greater failure. To get enmeshed in the lies and the deceit, the secrecy.

Sue

People in my life are surprised it's "still going on." I think they expect it should be done by now and, moreover, it would be done by now if it was happening in their house.

Sarah

This makes me so mad. It is very misconstrued. People think that girls with eating disorders just care about themselves... so many ideas that are completely wrong. It's nothing to do with that. There's so much people need to know. It's extremely complicated to explain to people, so that's why a lot of people just don't care to learn about because they can't understand it. I'm really glad that Dr. O does what she does 'cuz she struggled with it and is now helping girls with it.

• Body image, media and social media

Cassie

There's lots of teenaged girls that have body issues [that] they are not expressing. It is common in high school with girls. I think that has a lot to do with wanting to look perfect and have the guys to like them and stuff. Looks are everything in high school and I think that's where it starts. I think it needs to be shown more in school that it's okay to be yourself, at whatever size, because if someone actually loves you, they will be fine with what you look like.

Jack

I think we are sending a message to younger teenagers with some of the models about the perfect person. There is no perfect person. I think we as a society, we are too judgemental of what people look like, their size. But a lot of this eating disorders has a lot more to do with than just size. I honestly think it's more deep-rooted than that. When these poor kids lives are spinning out of control, it's their way of getting control. A lot of them don't intend for it to get that bad. It gets worse and it gets worse.

There are so many things that create an eating disorder, there's so many different triggers, it's marital breakdowns, there is sexual abuse, so many key triggers that set these poor girls off. I shouldn't say girls, there are boys too that get this illness.

Sandra

Oh, for sure, I think all the pressure to be thin and beautiful, to look perfect and the airbrushing they do with girls in magazines. Make them thinner, longer legs. There's a lot of pressure to be perfect.

Glenda

The obsession with—it's more dominant in girls, but even guys—having to be a certain way, and look a certain way and act a certain way, it's extremely difficult. There's a lot of peer pressure. It's not helpful. It's very unhealthy.

Cassie

A lot of people are going to blame the media, but I think for a lot of the girls, it was never something they saw on TV. That might have contributed to it, but for me, it was definitely the way I saw myself when I was five. I wish more was done for younger girls who were overweight or showing signs of not liking the way they looked. I wish they would be talked to, instead of teenaged girls. Because like I said, I was in the hospital when I was eight for something like this, and although I bounced right back and my parents probably never saw this coming, and neither did I, it planted an idea in my head and as soon as I was old enough to act upon it, and figure things out, I did.

Helen

I wonder whether that had an effect—the magazines? The models? I'm glad that there is now some real-sized models, if you want to call it that, on TV, on the programs. I also wonder... Julia had made a comment once...

one of her teachers at school had gone on her soapbox and was talking about the harmful effects of a certain type of condiment. Julia had come home and she was telling me all this and then I realized that Julia had stopped putting that condiment on her sandwich. Some people in society may not realize how influential they are, that something so silly can have a huge influence. I'm not saying this teacher is to blame. But it's in the back of my mind, this condiment story.

Sarah

I think it's important that teachers need to teach that a lesson, "Everyone's body looks different." 'Cuz their moms could be complaining that they are fat, and the kid is going to take after the mom. So the kids are at least shown at school: "No one looks the same. It's OK to look different." And that's just not happening.

Helen

Who knows whether it's the garment industry, you know? I never even knew there was a size zero!

Sue

Yeah, size zero. It's weird... ZERO? As in: doesn't exist? Girls so thin, they don't exist.

Julia

I don't know how we can prevent eating disorders from happening. Why is there an increased incidence of something like a mental health disorder? Is it because there are enhanced screening techniques and it's always been there? Or are people actually developing them more? I can't answer that. It's a very difficult question to answer.

Sarah

I watched this movie called *Misrepresentation* a couple of months ago and it's all about how women are portrayed. Like these women on magazine covers? That's altered, it's not real, it's not actually how their body looks, but girls see that and think, "I need to look like that". And it's an unreachable expectation, because it's fake. So they're constantly trying to reach this expectation which is unreachable, which is the first problem. And boys, are seeing those women and think that that's how women should look but women can't look like that 'cuz it's not real. And so they're constantly making fun of girls that don't look like celebrities and the girl is already self-conscious. It's all very scary and it's getting worse.

Sue

I find it really upsetting, now when there's a celebrity on the cover with bones sticking out everywhere and people are all going, "Oh! Isn't she beautiful!" I feel like screaming, "NO! that's an anorexic body. She's sick! Go up to 4F4, you'll see lots of girls who look just like that, attached to IV poles and feeding tubes in their noses."

Val

Ironically, it's the women who like thin women.

Hailey

That's kind of true.

Val

What happens in Grades 9, 10, 11... every little girl wants a boyfriend, to have the little prince and princess story. And girls think—and they perpetuate it in other girls—that the skinniest girl is the hottest girl. Whereas the guys, they really don't like that. They like girls that are normal weight or a little extra. So it's women doing this to other women. It's not necessarily men. Men get a bad rap, but it's not men, it's women.

Hailey

It's so screwed up.

Val

I was thinking about her friend from the Unit, when she was at her lowest and doing all those horrible things, she had a photo shoot where she was in a bikini and she put it on Facebook and everyone said how great she looked.

Hailey

She had her hospital 4F4 band on her arm.

Val

Everyone was saying, "Oh my god, you're so gorgeous".

Hailey

Things like that make it really hard.

Val

Oh my god... that is so damaging. For someone with an eating disorder, Facebook is the worst possible thing. I emailed her and said, "Pull that photo. Do you know how damaging that is to the girls on the Unit?"

Hailey

It's everywhere. It's everywhere.

Sue

I see girls posting pictures of themselves on Facebook. It's almost a compulsion: posting a new picture every day, waiting to see how many people will like it. How many people will tell them how beautiful they are. They are looking to Facebook for validation for their worth.

Hailey

So true. I even did that. And I'm 21.

Val

There were a couple of times in the past year that she took her Facebook right off and then she spent some time riding her horses.

Hailey

Yeah, I just knew I wasn't strong enough at the time, to take those triggers, so I would de-activate my Facebook until I felt like I could deal with it more. So that's a huge skill I've learned through DBT. It helped.

Val

Taking back control. These girls can take control; they can block. One of her ex-boyfriends, really was not helpful validating her, really not helpful at all. Finally, after two years, she blocked him... is that the right word?

Hailey

Well, I "unfriended" him, I haven't blocked him. So I'm half-way there.

Val

Well, block him next. That is real progress.

- **Don't make assumptions**

Cassie

I guess not to judge a person. Every person has a different story, different past, different experience. With eating disorders, they are all very different.

Jenn

Because people assume that you are throwing up, people are listening at the bathroom (even when the person is anorexic, not bulimic).

Rena

Don't just gloss over it, be aware that it can be very insidious. It's a very slippery slope. And don't just look at the outside. Things can be going on. You think the person looks so confident, so self-assured and they've got it all together. Don't just assume that that's the way it is. Everything is not the way you see it.

Val

One thing—just because you are thin, doesn't necessarily mean you have an eating disorder.

Hailey

And the other way around.

Val

Because I've been accused of having an eating disorder. "You're pretty thin..." I don't have an eating disorder. That's something that people don't understand. Hailey took a picture of herself at her normal goal weight and someone said, "Go eat." And that makes me so angry. Just because she's thin, and small—she is, she's always been small—doesn't mean she's sick. She's not sick right now. She's at her goal weight. She doesn't need to hear that: "Go eat." And bulimics are, often times, when they are recovering....

Hailey

A little bit overweight or normal weight.

Val

And they are so, so, so sick.

- **Ignorance in the medical world**

Jack

To be honest, in the medical system, I think they need to focus on it more, even when they are going through their schooling, they need to spend maybe a couple of weeks on an eating disorder ward so they have a better understanding. It's unbelievable that they are looking at this person, with her heart rate at 32 beats a minute, and they are saying, "What's wrong with her?" They don't understand.

Helen

That was one thing Julia said—when she was off in a bar with some friends and she fainted—in the emergency room, she told them that she has anorexia. And the nurses looked at her: "Oh, you're did this to yourself" and they walked away from her. She phoned me the next day to say this is what had happened. The nurses washed their hands of her because "Oh, you've done this to yourself. Smarten up, kid." But when you think about it, I can see their point of view. They have people with severe injuries come in, maybe there's car accidents or whatever, but she was there for a reason, they could have given her a little more empathy. It had an impact.

- **Support for parents**

Jack

I wish there was more information out there for parents. I know when Cassie was in the hospital, I wished there was a group that we could have gotten in contact with. So that you are able to communicate with other parents who are going through the same thing, because we didn't have that. I wish there was people we could have phoned and talked to.

Sandra

I think they need to have some sort of program for the family, too. I think they should have the family in for counselling. "Here are some pointers of what we feel is the best way to handle things." I never knew. Do I make her eat? Should I get mad if she doesn't eat, or do I just pretend I don't notice? What do you do? I don't know. I still don't know, to this day. I sort of wing it and hope for the best. That's a disappointment to me. Maybe they don't have the funding, I don't know.

[Supporting families] might make a big difference in recovery and how many girls relapse. They might find they get less girls back, if they train the family, help the families in how to support the girls better... and boys. That was really lacking and I still find that to be the case. A couple of times, Emma's had done something, maybe something a typical teen would do, but to me it's scary because it's Emma. She's more delicate to me. And I'll send a note, an email to Dr. O and she doesn't even respond to my emails. She doesn't send back a note and say, "No that's fine" or "That's something you need to deal with." Any kind of answer would be fine. She doesn't even acknowledge that I've sent her a note. She just ignores it. I find that hard.

Sue

So, do you think a parent support network would be helpful? Where you could ask for advice from other parents and professionals?

Sandra

Yes, that part was really lacking.

Glenda

I think parents could mentor parents, but it would be very complicated because a lot of people wouldn't willingly reveal... it's not that fun to sit and cry in front of a stranger. I guess you would get better at it. But, you know, as a survivor, you could....

Sue

Like all the cancer survivors who help other people going through treatment?

Glenda

Yeah, it might help. It's like anything. Some people are more open. You know, for me, I would go up to the Unit, but I didn't talk to anybody else and I just left. Even if somebody would've come and talked me— because I'm a really reserved, private person—I wouldn't probably have been that receptive. But not everyone is like that.

Even the few people that Sarah became a little bit closer to, even hearing Sarah talk about what their families are going through, was helpful. I think the idea of book is a good idea, personal interaction would be really good, it's just a really difficult thing to set up.

Since the interviews, the Eating Disorder Support Network of Alberta has been established by founder and President, Moyra McAllister. I serve as the Vice-President and, thanks to funding from the provincial government, support groups started being offered in the fall of 2014.

• Breaking through the shame, stigma & isolation

Helen

It's not a contagious disease. That child, or that young lady, or it could be a man I suppose, they still need you... don't be scared to eat in front of them. Be there. Still be a friend. You can still joke around with them. Even though they may put this wall up around them, don't give up. In a nutshell: don't give up on them. Don't just throw them away.

Ryan

Have you had anyone [lay] blame? That's one thing that's never happened here, no one has ever blamed. I'm very blessed because Kim could have easily said, "You did this. We know where this came from, we know what this is rooted in."

Kim

I think that's the biggest thing: the lack of conversation about mental health. And especially youth mental health. It's starting in the last couple of years. You start to hear more and more people coming out in the media saying they have suffered, but there still needs to be a lot more conversation.

Ryan

My best friend and I don't see each other anymore because his wife got diagnosed [with a mental illness] and I couldn't handle it. I walked away. I didn't want to see it anymore. I was done. Now, I see that it can be acknowledged, it can be treated, you can tell people.

Sue

I know one mother at the Unit who hasn't told her best friend that her daughter has been admitted. She just can't face it.

Kim

What does it say to your child? What they are going through has no value or that you are ashamed.

Ryan

If you come into work and say, "Guess what? I'm cancer free for three months!" Everyone goes, "Yeah!" But if you say, "Guess what? I'm bipolar and I dropped an ice-cream on the ground and I didn't cry or laugh." People are like, "Huh?" (*shrug*). But that's a huge thing. With my dad, if he dropped an ice cream cone you didn't know what he was going to do, he was either going to be so pissed off or he was going to be so happy. Which one is it? I think mental illness, especially amongst young people, is very prevalent and I think it gets misdiagnosed. You don't have a cast for anyone to sign, so it's not cool.

Kim

It's part of what drives kids underground. Why they need to lie and why it needs to be so hidden, because our world has forced them underground, forced it to be something that has to be hidden, by sweeping it under the carpet.

Ryan

Mental illness needs a Magic Johnson. Maybe Amanda Todd is Magic Johnson, because we are seeing the government actually having bullying conferences. It's sad to say we needed that. Maybe it can get more people talking.

Kim

We need a little more openness.

Ryan

And recognition. If it was cancer, or a broken leg, everyone would be running up to you, "What can I do for you? Oh my god, is he okay? Can I take the kids?"

Sue

I keep waiting for the casseroles. You know when something happens, people show up with casseroles? There have been no casseroles. Maybe people feel funny about bringing food because it's an eating disorder, but we still need to eat!

Kim

And your daughter would see that as support from the community.

Ryan

People spend too much thinking: "Oh, what will this mean?" Or "How will they feel that I know?" Rather than just jumping in.

Kim

As parents of kids who are struggling through it, we need to talk about it publicly. We need to put it out there. If you don't, your child sees it as something that you are ashamed of or that you are embarrassed and I don't think those are feelings that are helpful to them.

Ryan

If you were like: My daughter got her driver's license! She passed Math 30! But we don't want to talk about her eating disorder... that's not going to help at all. Instead, it all needs to be out there. That's part of her, that's all part of her. And there's so much good stuff. Just tons and tons.

RESEARCH SAYS

At the Institute of Cognitive Neuroscience Ruhr-Univeristät, scientists conducted fMRIs while people with anorexia looked at pictures of bodies. Scientists found that the anorexic brain has lower density of nerve cells in and poorer connectivity between the areas of the brain which are crucial for the perception of bodies. This may help to explain why people suffering from anorexia perceive themselves as fat.

Ruhr-Universität-Brochum (2013, January 24). "Connection Error" in brains of anorexics. *Science Daily.*
http://www.sciencedaily.com/releases/2013/130124091542.htm

Sue Huff
31 May 2013 · 👥

MRI results are in: it looks like a very tiny tumor indeed (1.3 cm). I'm pretty darn excited about this news, as all signs seem to indicate I will be able to avoid chemotherapy and just do radiation therapy! YUP, I'm doing the happy dance!! Oh yeah, oh yeah....

140 likes · 42 comments

👍 Like   💬 Comment   ➤ Share

Sue Huff
29 May 2013 · 👥

Letter arrived in the mail today from Alberta Foundation for the Arts (re: a grant for my book on families overcoming eating disorders). I was so convinced it was a rejection letter, I didn't open it and was bowled over when Kevin read it out loud to me tonight: "I am pleased to inform you that you've been awarded a grant..." wow!! I really needed...Continue Reading

106 likes · 36 comments

What breast cancer taught me about anorexia Part 2

The final gift of cancer was connection. Throughout Hannah's illness, I felt extremely isolated. It was the loneliness of her illness which propelled me to start this book, in fact. When I was diagnosed with breast cancer, I knew I couldn't survive in isolation any more, so I decided to reach out in a very public way. Within days of my diagnosis, I posted a message on Facebook letting everyone know. Throughout the journey, I continued to post updates (*post, above left*). The response was immediate and far-reaching. Hundreds of people commented, offered encouragement. I felt supported by many. And in the midst of all this, I received some good news about funding support for writing this book (*post, below left*).

On May 9, 2013, I was even mentioned in the Legislative Assembly of Alberta, by the Leader of the Opposition, Ms. Danielle Smith:

"Mr. Speaker, we got some disturbing health news last week from a former political colleague. Sue Huff, the former Leader of the Alberta Party, revealed that she has breast cancer. They've caught it early, so there is every reason to be hopeful, and I'm sure that we all wish Sue the very best. It's an appropriate time to raise the issue of a medical test that helps determine if chemotherapy is the appropriate course of treatment for a breast cancer patient. It's called Oncotype DX, and it's been reviewed and recommended by the Alberta breast cancer group and has also been approved for funding in Ontario, Quebec, Newfoundland, Saskatchewan, and Nova Scotia. Why isn't it available here?"

www.assembly.ab.ca, 28th Legislature, 1st Session

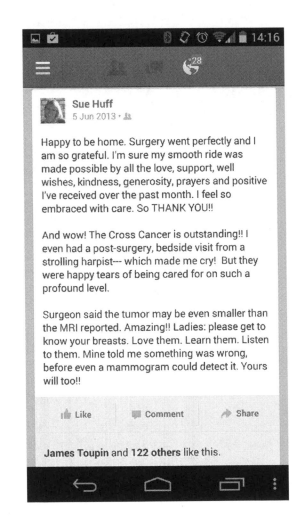

Sue Huff
5 Jun 2013 ·

Happy to be home. Surgery went perfectly and I am so grateful. I'm sure my smooth ride was made possible by all the love, support, well wishes, kindness, generosity, prayers and positive I've received over the past month. I feel so embraced with care. So THANK YOU!!

And wow! The Cross Cancer is outstanding!! I even had a post-surgery, bedside visit from a strolling harpist--- which made me cry! But they were happy tears of being cared for on such a profound level.

Surgeon said the tumor may be even smaller than the MRI reported. Amazing!! Ladies: please get to know your breasts. Love them. Learn them. Listen to them. Mine told me something was wrong, before even a mammogram could detect it. Yours will too!!

Like   Comment   Share

James Toupin and **122 others** like this.

...and by Minister of Health, Fred Horne:

"Mr. Speaker, Ms. Huff is a very good friend of many members on this side of the House as well, and we certainly wish her the very best with the challenge that she is facing...."

www.assembly.ab.ca, 28th Legislature, 1st Session

The truth is, the world came to me as soon as I asked for help. I felt my faith in community, in humanity, in friendship being restored and I realized that I am not alone. We are all connected. I belong to the tribe. I remember my step-father being overwhelmed by the outpouring of cards and letters he received when he was dying. He had no idea the number of lives he had touched and wryly commented, "It's a hell of way to find out." I think this is true for most of us. We are more cherished than we know and it takes a calamity for that to become clear (*post, left*).

So why did I lose sight of that connection in the previous year? Why did I feel so alienated and alone? I think part of it was I didn't make our family's struggle public, in part to respect Hannah's wish for privacy, in part to protect her because I wasn't sure how people would react. Many people didn't know about her diagnosis and those who did, weren't sure they were supposed to know, if they should tell anyone else, or what to do to be helpful. Because we weren't clear about our needs as a family, people didn't know how to respond. So, a lot of people just stayed away. Perhaps they were uncomfortable. Perhaps they thought we wanted privacy. Perhaps they had no idea how bad it was.

With my cancer diagnosis, I decided to spell it out: "This is happening. This is how I feel. Tell whoever you want. This is what I need right now." Being able to state exactly what I needed (company, distraction, food), made is easy for people to step up and deliver. I made a pledge to accept whatever help manifested, without judgement and I was surprised and delighted by who showed up. The truth is, some people can sit with bad news and others cannot. Some people have the time/energy/space in their lives to give, some people don't. It's hard when you feel certain people "should" be helping you, but, for whatever reason, they are absent. I tried very hard not to judge who was MIA, but simply accept that someone's ability to give has nothing to do my worthiness as the recipient. In fact, It has nothing to do with me, at all. When I reflect on the remarkable difference between the level of support I've felt during my treatment compared to the emptiness I felt during Hannah's treatment, I wonder how we might have done it differently.

It's very hard when your child doesn't want everyone to know, to find the balance between reaching out and protecting. Looking back, I think I could have been more clear and direct with the people who knew. I could have asked for more help, more specifically. But when you limit the pool of helpers to only family and close friends, you limit the help you will receive, especially with a long-term illness. Even if I had been direct, I don't think the small circle would have been able to meet the relentlessness of our needs.

And I wonder, at what point does "respecting someone's privacy" slip into "keeping a shameful secret?" I question now why we would need to hide the fact from anyone that our daughter was facing a critical illness. Did we unwittingly perpetuate the stigma? Getting sick isn't a crime. Needing help to overcome a serious illness isn't odd or unusual or wrong.

I wish now that I had continued to explore the issue of disclosure with Hannah and, with her permission, sent out a clear message to our friends and family. Something like this:

> Our beautiful, creative, intelligent daughter Hannah has been diagnosed with a very serious illness: anorexia nervosa. We are all struggling to understand and cope as she undergoes intensive treatment at the University of Alberta Eating Disorder Clinic. We have no idea how long it will take for her to recover but are so grateful that this program exists here in Edmonton so we can continue to be in close contact with her every day.
>
> Here's what we need at this point: prayers, kind words & cards of hope; meals for Kevin, Josh and me; grocery/errand runners; and daytime companionship for Sue (walks, coffee dates) in between hospital visits. Please note: Sue may need to leave suddenly if Hannah is struggling.
>
> It's likely that you know very little about eating disorders. Please take a minute to educate yourself, by visiting: www.nedic.ca. This will help clear

PHOTO: SUE HUFF

up any misconceptions you may have and help us connect at a time when we really need your support and understanding. Thanks!

So, while I wouldn't recommend getting cancer as a way to cope with eating disorders in your family (!!), it has certainly brought a lot of clarity for me. The truth is, I couldn't fully understand my daughter's battle to recover until I had to walk a similar path. I didn't understand the psychological and emotional aspects of anorexia until I felt the same fears and anxieties around cancer. I couldn't understand the many layers of guilt, blame, shame, stigma—until I had cancer to shine light on the dark corners. I couldn't understand how to truly support someone's recovery (as opposed to "taking it over") until I was the patient and felt that delicate balance myself. I couldn't let go, trust and ask for help, until I was given no other option.

In truth, I couldn't understand anorexia until I had cancer.

Now that I have completed all my treatments, people often congratulate me for fighting the good fight or beating cancer or "kicking its ass". Whenever they use this type of language, I feel like a fraud. The words don't fit and I feel like the compliment is for someone else. I haven't been fighting cancer. In fact, this may be the least "fight-y" thing I've ever done. I haven't been beating or kicking or pummeling. I've been releasing, accepting, acknowledging, sitting, resting, embracing, opening, moving, healing, expanding, experiencing, feeling, breathing, listening and wondering.

There is nothing to fight. Fear arises, fear subsides. Anger arises, anger subsides. Laughter arises, laughter subsides. Pain arises, pain subsides. Worry arises, worry subsides. Joy arises, joy subsides. Tears come, tears stop.

Hannah recently lost some weight, in a typical, dramatic fashion. Instantly, I felt the old familiars return: fear, despair, worry, frustration, anger. A turbulent, churning wave of emotions, full of foam and detritus crashed over me. My husband took the lead and calmly discussed a plan to restore the weight with our daughter. She agreed. Life rolled along.

The weight that she had lost in a week, she slowly and carefully gained again over three weeks. I realized that both the loss of weight and the restoration of weight needed to be treated with the same gentle equanimity. This is neither beginning nor end, neither the greatest or the worst, neither the highest or the lowest...

...it just *is*.

And, with love, this too shall pass.

Perhaps that is the hope I've been seeking all along.

now. So I guess this is the end of this journal & the start of a new one (green for growth.)
I feel sad & scared & unsure.
I want us all to be on dry land but it seems there is more swimming to do,
So, we swim.
Stroke, stroke, breathe
Stroke, stroke, breathe.
And, for the first time,
I notice how the water holds me
I don't need to fight so much.
I don't need to panic to stay afloat
The water has me.
And I feel it push me up.

Your story

I believe we all have the power to write our own story. The facts are the facts, but we choose which parts to emphasize and ultimately, we decide what it all means. So, draw, scribble, rage, reflect and build your own hope.

what's your story?

how do you build resilience?

what gives you hope?

Resources

Many of these recommendations come from *Practice Guideline for the Treatment of Patients with Eating Disorders* (Third Edition, 2006). This guideline is considered the gold standard for treatment, made available through the Psychiatric Practice section of the American Psychiatric Association website: **www.psych.org**

- **CBT-oriented workbooks and other approaches for self-help**

Agras, W.S. & Apple, R.F. (1997)
   Overcoming Eating Disorders: A Cognitive Behavioural Treatment for Bulimia Nervosa and Binge-Eating Disorder, Oxford University Press.

Albers, S. (2009)
   50 Ways to Soothe Yourself Without Food, New Harbinger Publications.

Cash, T.F. (1997)
   The Body Image Workbook: An 8-Step Program for Learning to Like Your Looks, New Harbinger Publications.

Costin, C. & Schubert Grabb, G. (2012)
   8 Keys to Recovery from an Eating Disorder, Effective Strategies from Therapeutic Practice and Personal Experience, W.W. Norton and Company.

Fairburn, C. (1995)
Overcoming Binge Eating, Guilford.

Goodman, L.J. & Villapiano, M.
Eating Disorders: The Journey to Recovery Workbook

Schmidt U. & Treasure, J.
Getting Better Bit(e) by Bit(e): A Survival Kit for Sufferers of Bulimia Nervosa and Binge Eating Disorder

- ## Other books reported to be helpful by patients/families

Anderson, A.E., Cohn, L. & Holbrook, T. (2000)
Making Weight: Men's Conflicts with Food, Weight, Shape and Appearance, Gürtze Books.

Bulik, C.M. & Taylor, N. (2005)
Runaway Eating: The 8-Point Plan to Conquer Adult Food and Weight Obsessions, Rodale.

Ellis, A. / Abrams & M./Dengelegi, L. (1992)
The Art and Science of Rational Eating, Barricade Books.

Hall, L. (1993)
Full Lives: Women Who Have Freed Themselves From Food and Weight Obsessions, Gürtze Books.

Lock, J. & le Grange, D. (2005)
Help Your Teenager Beat an Eating Disorder, Guilford.

Michel, D.M. & Willard S.G. (2003)
When Dieting Becomes Dangerous, Yale University Press.

Rutledge (2007)
Skills-based Learning for Caring for a Loved One with an Eating Disorder: The New Maudsley Method, Routledge.

Siegel, M., Brisman, J. & Weinshel, M. (2009)
Surviving an Eating Disorder, Strategies for Families and Friends, Collins Living.

Walsh, B.T. & Cameron, V.L. (2005)

> *If Your Child Has an Eating Disorder: An Essential Resource for Parents*,
> Guilford.

Zeckhausen, D. (2008)

> *Full Mouse, Empty Mouse, A Tale of Food and Feelings*,
> Magination Press.

Zerbe, K. (2005)

> *The Body Betrayed: A Deeper Understanding of Women, Eating*
> *Disorders and Treatment*, Gürtze Books.

- **Internet resources**

Academy of Eating Disorders
> **www.aedweb.org**

Eating Disorder Referral and Information Center
> **www.edreferral.com**

Eating Disorder Support Network of Alberta (EDSNA)
> **www.eatingdisordersupportnetworkofalberta.com**

Families Empowered and Supporting Treatment for
Eating Disorders (FEAST)
> **www.feast-ed.org**

National Association of Anorexia and Associated Disorders
> **www.anad.org/site/anadweb**

National Eating Disorders Association
> **www.nationaleatingdisorders.org**

National Eating Disorder Information Centre of Canada (NEDIC)
> **www.nedic.ca**

Something Fishy
> **www.somethingfishy.org**

PHOTO: PENNY WOODING

Postscript

Sue has celebrated her one-year cancer-free milestone. She feels very healthy and is happy to be working, volunteering with EDSNA and laughing more. Her daughter Hannah is successfully maintaining a healthy weight, enjoying high school and embracing new challenges.

Both Sue and Hannah continue to be supported and closely monitored by their medical teams.

About the author

Sue Huff lives in Edmonton, Alberta, Canada with her husband and their two teenaged children. She has always been drawn to telling people's stories and has written for radio, television, theatre and film. She has received several awards for her writing and is particularly proud of a short film she wrote and directed for the National Film Board of Canada called *Kids Talkin' About Death* and a docu-comedy television series she wrote for the LIFE Channel about gender differences called *Who's On Top?* She co-wrote a play about female body image in 1992, several years before her daughter was born.

Sue has also worked as an actor, a politician and a community advocate. She loves singing, sailing, gardening, reading, swimming and travelling.

She considers walking the path of anorexia with her daughter, by far, the hardest thing she has ever done.

This is her first book.

Made in the USA
Charleston, SC
20 April 2015